BACKPACKING
IN THE
MIDDLE EAST
AND
AFRICA

MARTHA MARINO

iUniverse LLC
Bloomington

BACKPACKING IN THE MIDDLE EAST AND AFRICA

iUniverse books may be ordered through booksellers or by contacting:

iUniverse LLC
1663 Liberty Drive
Bloomington, IN 47403
www.iuniverse.com
1-800-Authors (1-800-288-4677)

ISBN: 978-1-4917-0189-8 (sc)
ISBN: 978-1-4917-0190-4 (e)

Library of Congress Control Number: 2013914011

Printed in the United States of America

iUniverse rev. date: 09/25/2013

CONTENTS

OPENING & BASIC PREMISE

This book tells about my travels in the Middle East and Africa. I had many unique experiences which I thought others might be interested in reading about. On my trips I always keep a journal and take pictures. When I return home I put them in a book.

This book will take you to some unusual places. In Ankara I tell about Ataturk's mausoleum, in Konya, Rumi's museum, then to some Roman ruins, and gorgeous beaches. In Israel I mention the famous places like Dome of the Rock, the Holy Sepulchre church and my funky hotel in Jaffa. I mention crossing the Suez Canal and the famous places to see in Cairo. Then in Africa I tell about taking a bus around South Africa, riding in a mokoro (canoe) on the Okawanga Delta in Botswana and climbing the sand dunes in Nambia. These experiences were unforgettable and am sure you'll enjoy reading about them.

SECTION I
MIDDLE EAST

THE MIDDLE EAST

Map of the middle east where I travled

PART 1

ANKARA

My Middle East trip began in Turkey. Since I'd been to Istanbul several times, I flew direct to Ankara. At the airport, for an easy and cheap ride into the city, I piled into a local bus. Soon I discovered, though, that none of the passengers spoke English or any of the other languages I know.

What was worse, no one had every heard of the Engen Hotel where I planned to stay. Without a clue of where to get off, I just kept circling the city until I was the only one left on the bus.

Finally, the driver stopped and pointed to the door. I got the hint. Grabbing my heavy backpack, I climbed down. I had no idea where I was. All I could see were the surrounding brown fields and a nearby three story, concrete building . . . . Only later I learned that the central bus station was on the ground floor of the concrete building. Weary from my 16 hour flight, I reminded myself that the first day of a trip is the toughest. "It's bound to get better," I mumbled.

Wishing a taxi—or anyone for that matter—would rescue me, I waited by the curb.

After a while an old sedan drove up; luckily, it was a taxi. I showed the driver the name of the Engen Hotel. Nodding, he indicated that he knew exactly where it was. "How much will it cost?" I inquired cautiously. Without one word, he simply pointed to the meter. Assuming that everything was under control, I opened the door and sat down.

As we cruised through the city, with the meter ticking away, familiar monuments popped up, like the equestrian statue of Ataturk sitting high on his bronze horse right in the middle of a roundabout. Was I on another city tour? I wondered anxiously. Soon we turned onto the busy six-lane Ataturk Bulvari (Boulevard). Suddenly ignoring the cars behind, the driver stopped in the right lane and pointed to the door. Not again! I thought. I could see no hotel in sight—only fancy shops and streams of pedestrians walking on the sidewalk. While horns blasted and motorists shouted angry words, that luckily I couldn't understand, a lengthy sign-language session ensued between us. I got the idea that somewhere in the vicinity sat my hotel. Since it was situated on a one-way street, he motioned I'd have to walk. I only prayed this didn't mean I would end up at the bus station again.

The taximeter indicated that I owed thousands of Turkish Lira (there were 500.000 to one dollar). I handed over a stack of bills with so many zeros on them that it looked like I was paying the national debt. But instead of being pleased, the driver shook his head and shoved them back into my hand. What's up? I wondered, thoroughly confused. Hadn't the driver already driven me all over town—instead of taking a direct route? And now he wanted extra money? What nerve! As horns honked louder and the traffic jam grew in size, all I wanted to do was escape. Finally, like in a game of cards, I spread out all the money I had exchanged—a hundred dollar's worth—and said sarcastically, "O.K, it's your turn, you choose!" Watching millions of Turkish lire disappear from my hand made my heart sink. "Weren't things supposed to get better?" I grumbled, watching the taxi disappeared. Only later did I understand what actually happened. Since taximeters don't show all the zeros (because there are too many), it was quite possible that the driver hadn't over charged me at all. Who knows? Nonetheless, it was expensive taxi ride—about 26$.

For a while, I wandered around looking for my hotel. The taxi driver was right. It was on a narrow, one way street and difficult to find.

The Engen Hotel was a friendly place. It had a large curbside terrace where I ate a Turkish breakfast every morning. Usually it consisted of crinkly, black, bitter olives, salty goat cheese, crunchy toast and, sometimes, a hard-boiled egg and tomato slices. Ugh! I would have preferred delicious Turkish coffee, but it's usually drunk after a main meal and not for breakfast.

The following day I planned to rest and recuperate from jet lag. But since I couldn't sleep, I got up and rode a bus to one of Ankara's famous sights: the Antolian Civilization Museum. Here I learned about Turkey's long, historical past. The displays began with the Hittites—who had a few "run-ins" with the Egyptians around 2000 BC. They were followed by a string of other civilizations like the: Persians, the Greeks, the Romans, the Byzantines, the Seljuk's and the Ottomans. Having been the main stage for so many civilizations, Turkey has ancient ruins on almost every corner.

From the museum, I hiked up the hill. Behind a tall, thick stonewall, stood the *hizar* (fortress) built by the Byzantines in about 600 AD. While strolling through the cobble stone streets, I discovered an elegant, terrace restaurant, overlooking red-roofed houses and the surrounding hills. I don't usually eat in expensive restaurants, but feeling travel weary, I decided to treat myself. "I'll just have an eggplant salad (*Patlikan*)," I said to the waiter, wanting something Turkish to eat.

When it came, though, it didn't resemble a salad at all. "What's that?" I asked, pointing to a glob of beige-colored puree on my plate.

"*Patlikan*." Then he motioned for the headwaiter to come and explain in English, that, without a lettuce leaf, it really was a "salad".

It had a strong garlic flavor and with the help of plenty of toast and mineral water, I finish most of it. Since *Patlikan* is on every Turkish menu, I was glad I tried it at least once.

The next tourist sight I visited was Ataturk's mausoleum: a huge rectangular monument with square columns, guarded by high stepping soldiers dressed in blue and white uniforms. It was extremely impressive and gave a feeling of the greatness of Ataturk, known as the father of the nation. After WW1 and the demise of the Ottoman Empire, Ataturk saved the country from being carved up by the Western nations. He fought courageously against the allies and renegotiated the treaties. Then, in 1923, he established the Turkish Republic.

While President for fifteen years, Ataturk accomplished many important things: He separated the government from religion—removing Islam as the State religion; replaced the Arabic alphabet with a modified Latin one, so people could read more easily; adopted a constitution which gave women the right to vote and lastly required everyone to take a last name. Some problems, though, still exist between the orthodox Muslims and the government. In *The Turkish Daily News,* an English language newspaper, I read that one afternoon some strict, orthodox Islamic women harassed and threw things at women employees as they were leaving the ministry of education. Why? "Because their arms were uncovered!"

I stayed in Ankara for three days. Then—by direct route, this time—returned to the bus station to catch a bus to Goreme, known for its fantastic stone formations.

PART 2

GOREME & KONYA

Endless stretches of golden brown wheat fields flashed by my window as our Kapadokya Bus rolled along a deserted, two lane highway from Ankara. It was a pleasant four-hour trip with superb service: all the way a smiling young boy poured perfumed water into my hands and brought me free drinks and snacks.

When the bus reached Nevsehir, a van was waiting to take Kamara, a Japanese man in his 50's, and me to Goreme. It's a village in Cappadocia of weird-shaped tufa columns (soft porous stone) caused by the eruptions thousands of years ago from three distant volcanoes.

I had hoped that Kamara would know of a good pension in Goreme, but all he had was the same list as I from the *Lonely Planet Guide*. Our driver, a kind soul who understood our dilemma, volunteered to drive us around. I wanted to stay in a pension with "cave rooms" hacked out of tufa, but when I realized how musty they smelled, I changed my mind. Finally, we settled for rooms at the SOS Pension. It proved to be a good choice. Nestled against a hill at the end of the village, it had a wonderful, whitewashed terrace. It overlooked a valley of exotic shaped pinnacles, formed by hardened ash that had been eroded by wind, rain and rocks. If boulders were sitting on top of them, they were called "fairy chimneys".

I liked my small, roof-top room. It was covered with deep crimson, oriental carpets on the walls, floor and bed—so comfortable it was like being in a lover's arms.

And from my front window I had a million dollar view: I gazed upon a dramatic lunar landscape of strange tufa formations, all for fifteen dollars a night! My days in Goreme were leisurely and quiet. After the blazing sunrays seeped from the sky, I would stroll in the late afternoon through green valleys hidden among the mushroom-like columns. Here, I'd see peasant women busily digging in vegetables plots or picking grape leaves for an evening meal—their donkeys tied nearby. Later, in the evening's balmy air, other pension guests and I sauntered into the small village. From an outside restaurant we'd watch farmers returning in their donkey-drawn carts from a day in the fields and hear prayer calls amplified by loud speakers from nearby mosques. We'd first drink a couple of beers, then order dinner. It always began with an appetizer (*meze*) that we selected from a glass case near the kitchen. My favorite one was stuffed eggplant; called *iman beijiter* and translated "the monk fainted" because it tasted so sumptuous. For our second course, we usually ate fish or shish kebab. Turkish cuisine I found delicious.

Goreme, though only a farming community, was invaded daily by busloads of tourists. They came to see its famous Open Air Museum, an area of hundreds of concealed churches and monasteries carved out of tufa cliffs. To avoid being slaughtered by the Romans and later the Muslims, the early Christians hid inside them. Some of the churches' interiors, from the 7th, 8th and 9th centuries, were decorated with Byzantine frescos depicting Christ's life and his miracles. The newly restored ones were exquisite.

To visit the many sites around Cappadocia, I joined an organized tour from Goreme. Our first stop was at Derinkuju, an underground city. Here people lived off and on for over 2000 years to hide from invaders or religious persecutors. Because of the soft volcanic soil, they were able to dig down as far as 80 feet or eight layers. Inside was a labyrinth of small rooms with airshafts, wells, tunnels and even a winery. "Boozing it up" may have been the secret of their survival in these dark, austere conditions. Who knows? At another tour stop, we entered a restored Caravanerai, sort of an 800-year-old Motel Six for camel herders. They could pull in here for a safe night. Behind its high, thick walls and majestic carved portal were all the comforts a camel herder could dream of, except maybe swirling belly dancers. It had barns, dormitories, canteens and even a two-story, square-shaped mosque for prayers.

Along the old Turkish trade routes, other caravanserais ruins can still be seen. They are usually about 40 kilometers apart, a day's camel ride if all went well.

It was hard to leave the sleepy, little village of Goreme with its extraordinary tufa scenery. But after five days, I hopped on a bus to visit Konya. I wanted to see the capital of the powerful Seljuk civilization, of the 12th & 13th centuries, and the burial place of Rumi, a revered mystical poet who began the whirling dervishes.

I learned about Rumi (called Mevlana in Turkey) from my Afghanistan and Iranian friends whom I met at Divers Cove in Laguna Beach. While lying in the warm sand, they used to read out loud Rumi's poems; so ethereal they'd send me for hours spinning on the edge of reality.

Upon my arrival in Konya, I headed directly for Rumi's mausoleum. The interior was breathtaking. Every inch, from floor to ceiling, was decorated in rich red and gold arabesque. A thick velvet shroud of gold embroidery covered Rumi's coffin and a symbolic turban sat on top. Wearing a full-length borrowed smock, I followed the other visitors on their pilgrimage. In front of the Great Sage's tomb, reverently I bowed and kneeled. While praying, something magical happened to me: I felt a deep sense of peace descend over me. It truly is a holy place.

Konya, in addition to its religious importance, was filled with many ancient Seljuk ruins and mosques. In spite of this, though, few foreign visitors were on the streets. In fact, I seemed to be the only one. I wasn't lonely, though. The ubiquitous carpet vendors kept me company. They were easy to meet. They always stood in front of their open-faced shops and lured me inside with offers of hot apple tea. Sometimes they were pushy fellows but usually entertaining: One played his guitar while his friend danced a Turkish jig; another explained to me Konya's history and the third told me about his trip through Bulgaria on the way to his shop in Milan. "I used to drive through Yugoslavia," he explained, "but now with the trouble in Kosovo, it's too dangerous."

Of all the shopkeepers I met, Kamil was my favorite. A stocky, middle-aged man, whose deep black eyes pleaded for romance. He enticed me "among his carpets" with a dinner invitation. While serving me pizza (*etli ekmek*a) and a yogurt drink (*ayran*), his assistant laid out carpet after carpet at my feet. They <u>were</u> very beautiful, but admirably I resisted handing over my visa card. Instead, I steered our conversation to stories about Kamil's life.

He told me: his mother was a strict Muslim who always wore a long coat and scarf in public, that his uncle taught him the carpet business and that he had an arranged marriage.

"Why was that?" I inquired curiously, thinking he had the stamp of a modern European man.

"It was the easiest way to find a bride," he answered. "Besides, I thought my Mother's judgment was the best."

How I wish my sons felt that way!

PART 3

OLYMPUS

Olympus Beach Turkey

When I flew into Turkey, I never intended to go to Olympus, but all the tourists I met raved about the place. "You'll love the beach there," they exclaimed. "And you can stay in a tree house at the Orange Pension. It's only four dollars a night, including breakfast and dinner."

The more I heard about this bargain, the more intrigued I became. "How do I get there?" I finally asked. "Just take a bus from Antalya and ask the driver to drop you off along the road near Olympus. You'll *probably* find a van waiting to take you to the Pension." The word "probably" bothered me. "What about an address or phone number?" "Oh, you won't need that. Everyone knows where the Orange Pension is." These vague directions worried me, of course, but I couldn't resist a resort that sounded like paradise. Besides, I was use to sacrificing security for adventure. So, instead of heading for the Aegean as I had planned, I hopped on a bus for the Mediterranean. The six-hour ride from Konya was a pleasant trip . . . past serene, sapphire-blue lakes and pine-covered mountains. None of the passengers, however, knew a word of English. I managed, though. I discovered two Turks who spoke German. They had gone to German schools when their parents worked in Germany as *gastarbeiters* (guest workers). In fact, I used to have some Turkish students in my classes when I taught in Germany.

What an interesting surprise! After we pulled into Antalya, I transferred to a small bus that supposedly passed by the road to Olympus, or at least that's what I understood from a ticket vendor who only spoke Turkish.

Sitting on the bus were two other tourists: a young Chinese girl from Singapore named Joyce and her English boyfriend, David, a cyclist who had just ridden his bike all the way from India to Turkey. Imagine! They were also camping at Olympus and confirmed its spectacular beauty. "What's the Orange Pension like?" I asked, thinking they'd know where it was. "The what?" they responded with surprise. "We've never heard of it."

A pang of disappointment shot through me like an arrow. How could that be possible? Didn't everyone know about the Orange Pension? "We get off near Cirali," David added. "Maybe your stop is further down the road." With dusk seeping from the sky and fearing I might become stranded, I wasn't about to find out. So when Joyce and David got off the bus, I joined them. "I'll look for the Orange Pension once I arrive," I said, consoling myself.

A taxi was supposed to be waiting on the road to take us 13 km to the beach. But none was in sight. Without a choice we began hitchhiking.

Night crept around us as we waved at passing cars. At last, a driver in a Mercedes picked us up. In broken English, he explained that his motel was only part way down the road, which meant we'd have to walk the rest of the way to the beach. Under an ink black sky, we trudged along the remaining kilometers, stopping occasionally to ask if anyone had heard of the Orange Pension. "No" was always the answer. Resigned to my fate and ignoring my surge of disillusion, I checked in at the Yavuz Pension, a comfortable place that served a copious Turkish breakfast. The next morning I hurried to the beach. After one glance, I understood why my friends had raved about Olympus. It was breathtaking. Green carpeted mountains rose majestically in the background and rocky cliffs jetted into the water at the end of a crescent-shaped bay. The blue Mediterranean, in the fresh morning sunlight, sparkled like diamonds. A quiet, serene feeling hung in the air.

For a while, I strolled happily along the pebbled beach (also a reserve for sea turtles) and, believe it or not, finally met another tourist who actually knew where the Orange Pension was. "Go to the end of the beach," he explained, "and follow a path inland for about a mile. You can't miss it."

Excited about the news, I rushed to the trail which led me through the Olympus National Park. Ancient tombs and aqueducts from a Lycian city (2 BC) and a Roman settlement (1AD) lined the path. Then it edged along the banks of a stream through a narrow, rocky gorge with thick verdure. At last, I came to a shady open café. It was the Orange Pension. Sitting at tables people— some the hippy-type—were chatting with friends or writing letters, while a few lounged in hammocks nearby. The feeling of "anything goes" permeated the air. I sat down at an empty table and ordered a cup of apple tea. Shortly, a young, chubby Japanese girl joined me. "I love this place," she bubbled excitedly. "It's my second time here." Her name was Kamara, and she worked in L.A, making commercials for TV stations in Japan. "The Japanese like to see beautiful, blond girls on California beaches," she said. Later Kamara showed me her tree house. Snuggle among orange trees, it was a primitive, one room, wooden shack, built on stilts with a ladder leading to the front veranda. It would have been a novel place to stay. However, I liked the Yavuz Pension near the sea and didn't want the trouble of moving. For almost a week, I lounged around the tranquil beach at Olympus, swimming in the salty Mediterranean, reading books under thatch-roof umbrellas and dining in the beachside cafes with my new-made friends. Everyday I postponed my departure. I couldn't imagine ever finding such an idyllic place again. Besides, I dreaded hitchhiking back to the main highway and waiting for a bus that had no schedule. To my surprise, though, my departure day turned out to be terrific. It began at the local store café in front of a narrow dirt road. Here I sat waving at all the passing cars. Finally, a motel owner offered to take me to the main highway. There, after waiting in the boiling midday sun for over a half an hour, a shinny, green sedan screeched to a halt beside me.

"Where are you going?" a young man with black bushy hair, shouted. "To Kas"

"Hop in! We're going there, too."

Without hesitating, I slung my backpack into the back seat and sat down in his luxurious, air-conditioned car with Turkish folk music oozing out of the stereo. "My name is Junet," he announced, "and this is my wife, Eepak. We're on our honeymoon from Ankara." Junet, a journalist, was a super kind of guy—fun and free-spirited. We investigated all the tourist sites along the way and picked up anyone who needed a ride. Our first stop was at Myra, known for its large, impressive Roman amphitheater and Lycian rock tombs. Carved into the hillside, they resembled small houses.

Next, we visited the 3rd century church of St. Nicolas. It was built in honor of a Byzantine monk, named St. Nicolas, famous for giving presents to children and the needy. Who'd ever imagine that our Santa Claus legend originated in Turkey!

Later, we picked up a young fisherman. Following his special recommendation, we drove an extra 25 km to a quaint fishing village just for a fresh fish lunch. Then afterwards, we hired a private yacht (big enough for 30 people). We wanted to see the Lycian's sunken city below Kekova island and swim in the clear blue water.

As twilight faded, we arrived in Kas where Junet stopped at a cliff-side hotel to look for rooms and bargain for a good price. I had already watched him bargain for the biggest fish in the restaurant and the largest yacht in the harbor. Now, he began haggling with the desk clerk, then the manager and at last the owner. With everyone standing around, you'd think Junet was trying to buy the hotel. But thanks to his expertise, I had a great room with a beautiful view of the surrounding hills and islands in the Mediterranean. The price? Only twelve dollars a night including two sumptuous meals a day. I couldn't believe I had found another resort I never wanted to leave.

PART 4

KAS, FETHIYE, MARMARIS, ICMELER & SELJUK

Kas, a village steeped in quiet beauty, was the pearl of the Mediterranean. Green hills framed its island-filled bay and chalky white cliffs lined the water's edge. Staying in Kas was so wonderful I felt that life's worries were put on hold. Daily, in the warm sunshine, I'd lounge on one of the cliff-side terraces. Then I'd swim in the cool, refreshing water, enjoy snacks and drinks served by an attentive waiter and chat with friendly lounge-chair neighbors, an elderly couple from Germany and a pretty flight attendant from Istanbul.

After dinner, my ideal life continued. In the evening's warm, velvety air, I'd take a stroll to the main square and browse in the artistic shops. My favorite one sold handicrafts and peasant jewelry from Turkmenistan, a country across the Caspian Sea, formally a part of the Soviet Union. Once, while I was trying on a heavy peasant, silver necklace, the supply merchant arrived from his country. He was a short, dark skinned man with a round face and slanting eyes. I would have liked to talk to him about life in Turkmenistan, but no one could translate for me. I had heard from two Peace Corps volunteers stationed there, that the country had not wanted its independence. But since it was so poor, the Soviet

Union wouldn't allow it to remain in their union. I wondered if that were true.

My next stop along the Mediterranean was Fethiye, a small, busy port about three hours away. It was an easy trip. Most of the time the driver and I were the only ones on the bus. The difficult part was finding a place to stay once I arrived. At first, I took a taxi to the Ideal Pension. But it turned out to be anything but ideal. With its tiny, funky rooms, its dusty outdoor, rooftop lounge and creepy manager, it was the last word in discomfort. I knew I couldn't stay there, so I walked toward the harbor and found a suitable two star hotel, called the Otel Dedeoglu. Here I had an air-conditioned room with breakfast, a TV and a view of the boats coming and going for only seven dollars a night. A real bargain! The shortage of tourists in Turkey brought the prices down. Because of the political situation, many Europeans had cancelled their trips. Ocalen, the "top dog" of the Kurds, had landed in prison. Defiantly, he announced that if he were condemned to death—which happened after my arrival—he'd have his terrorists bomb the "hell" out of the tourist resorts. A reasonable threat to scare cautious tourists away, right? Being courageous or stupid—either one—I ignored the travel warnings, which I had done once before . . . and survived. In 1987, in spite of the Chernobyl nuclear disaster I traveled to the Soviet Union. I took the Trans Siberian Express from Beijing and had a fabulous trip! With only a few passengers on board, I practically had the entire first-class car—and the attendants—all to myself! This time, by ignoring Ocalen's bully tactics, I was enjoying a bargain-priced vacation. Anyway flirting with danger adds to the adventure.

While in Fethiye, I took the famous twelve-island boat trip. We cruised the entire day among small islands, stopping in picturesque, sandy coves for a relaxing swim. Usually we moored next to luxurious, chartered yachts that tourists leased to sail around the coast from Mamaris to Antalya. I would have liked to take one of these super weeklong cruises. Unfortunately, though, I was always headed in the wrong direction! After Fethiye, I left the Mediterranean Sea for the Aegean to see its spectacular coast. I knew the famous resort of Mamaris would be expensive, so I planned to stay in a neighboring town.

"You'll love Icmeler!" my friends exclaimed. "It's a small resort and really beautiful." In Mamaris, after visiting its immense covered bazaar and hilltop fortress, I jumped into a water-taxi for a twenty-minute ride across the scenic bay to Icmeler.

As we pulled into the Icmeler's harbor, nestled below the mountains, I couldn't believe my eyes. It wasn't a small resort at all. Its shores were lined with at least fifty super costly hotels and rows and rows of yellow umbrellas and white plastic lounge chairs. Dazed and disappointed, I stood motionless on the pier. A fellow passenger, noticing my state of shock, asked which hotel I was looking for. "I don't have a cue," I replied, "I'm an 'unpackaged' tourist." My answer probably surprised him. Most visitors in Turkey are on arranged tours. I couldn't afford to stay in a large, high-priced hotel. Not knowing what to do, I shuffled toward the beach. On the sand, I found some scarf-covered, peasant ladies, renting beach chairs and selling fruit. Feeling hungry, I bought one of their succulent peaches and then with sign language, indicated that I would like to leave my heavy backpack with them for a while. With friendly smiles, they agreed.

Before hotel hunting, I stopped at a café for a quick snack—food always improves my unhappy moods. Afterwards, I walked through the side streets. Finally, I found a moderate-sized hotel. Using my new bargaining skills, the ones I learned from Junet in Kas, I haggled about the price. After a lengthy discussion with manager and desk clerk, I got a front-balcony room for a reasonable price. I know Junet would have been proud of me.

I stayed in Icmeler for a few days and eventually liked the busy resort. While swimming, I made friends with two young English girls who were so madly in love with Turkish men, that I wished I were young again, too. One boyfriend was a cute waiter in a local cafe and the other a handsome veterinarian who told me a lot about his life in Istanbul. He said his mother wanted him to have an arranged marriage, but he preferred English girls. "Turkish women are too restricted," he complained. After Icmeler I left the coast and took a bus to Seljuk. I wanted to visit Ephesus, the world's best-preserved Roman city and the former capital of their Asia Minor province. It was only 3km from Seljuk. In spite of the blazing sun, I spent hours wandering around its fascinating ancient ruins. Among the sites were the huge 25,000-seat theater, where St. Paul lectured to the Ephesians to mend their errant ways, the marble street lined with pillars that led to the harbor—which has since silted up, and the magnificent Celsus library. This was built in the 2nd century AD by the son of the Julius Celsus, once a governor of Asia Minor.

Decorated with friezes and statues, the library's two rows of Corinthian, marble columns were so perfectly proportioned that looking at them, gave me a sense of beauty and harmony. No wonder the library's picture is on the cover of most Turkish brochures. In addition to these Roman ruins, Seljuk had several famous Christian sites. One was the remains of the Basilica of St

John. It was built in honor of John the apostle who lived here while writing his Gospel. The other was the house where Virgin Mary died. St. John brought her to Turkey after the death of Jesus.

How surprising that Turkey played an important role in Christianity!

The Celus Library in Ephesus

PART 5

PAMUKKALE

Before leaving Turkey I wanted to see Pamukkale's dazzling white limestone pools advertised in every travel folder. Since they were near Seljuk, where I was staying, I just jumped in a tourist van, and in less than three hours I was there. By walking around Pamukkale, I found a small, yellow pension, called the Weisse Berg (<u>white</u> mountain). Here I lounged around its shady pool until the sweltering heat subsided. Then about five o'clock, I started my hike up the white limestone hill on the outskirts of the village which looked like a ski slope sitting in a green field. When I reached the terraced pools, once formed by calcium deposits from volcanic springs, I felt as if I were looking at a fairytale landscape. The pale blue water in the snow-white basins glistened in the sunlight. It was breathtaking. Though I enjoyed hiking up these scenic travertines, it was difficult. Nobody was allowed to wear shoes, or step inside them, where the surface was smooth. We had to stay along their rough edges. When my feet began to scream with pain, I'd put on my shoes or wade in the pool's warm, shallow water. If an inconspicuous guard saw me, tip-toeing around the rules, he'd blow his shrill whistle at me. Rather embarrassing to be singled out. At the top of the 400-foot plateau stood the ruins of an ancient city called the Hieropolis, built about 1800 years ago. The Romans were excellent city planners: they placed their large Stone temples right next to hot bubbling mineral springs.

I strolled past the huge, square stone pillars to the adjacent municipal spa, once called the Sacred Pond. Just like Cleopatra, who was rumored to have bathed here, I floated in its knee-high thermal pools. Unlike in former times, the marble columns were no longer decorating the pool's edge. They were on the bottom in fragments, scratching my feet. Repeated earthquakes had tumbled them down.

After a few days of enjoying thermal swims and home cooked meals at the Weisse Berg, I rode the bus directly to Izmir to catch a plane to Israel. I had been in Turkey a month and felt sad to leave. I knew I'd miss its friendly people, beautiful beaches and ancient ruins.

PART 6

TEL AVIV

My flight to Tel Aviv was late. For hours I sat in a crowded waiting room, listening to announcements in Turkish, that I couldn't understand. Finally, I got tired of not knowing what was going on. I walked over to a group of people and spoke to one of the large, gray haired women. "Do you speak English?" I inquired politely. She smiled and shook her head.

Since I used to be a foreign language teacher, I tried again. "*Sprechen Sie Deutsch*? I asked. Another shake of the head.

Next I questioned if she knew French. The same negative response. Just for fun, even though I was "batting zero", I continued. "*Habla espanol*? To my utter amazement, she replied, "*Si*". What a shock! Even though her pronunciation was different from mine, we could converse together. I learned that she lived in Israel and came to Turkey to see her relatives and tour the Black Sea. When I asked how she knew Spanish (known as Ladino), she patiently gave me a history lesson: "My ancestors came from Spain. During the inquisition in 1492 (that's when the all Jews were expelled) they immigrated to Izmir. I'm what you call a sephardic Jew," I found it amazing, that after so many years, her main language was still Spanish and not Turkish or Hebrew. On the plane we sat next to one another. When I was ready to give my snack tray back to the flight attendant, she did an amusing thing: She took my unused salt and pepper packages and handed them to me. "You may need these," she said in Spanish. I appreciated her motherly interest but wondered if her frugality was an inborn Jewish trait.

It was about eight o'clock when we arrived in Tel Aviv. After fighting my way through crowds and customs, I went to the reservations office to ask for help. Having heard that Israel was more expensive than the States, I wanted to avoid landing in a high-priced, ocean front hotel. A lady at the counter listened to my request and phoned many guest houses, but at such a late hour all were full. "What should I do?" I asked, feeling I was about to sink in the murky waters of despair She thought a moment. "I guess you'll have to stay in Jaffa." "Where's that?" "On the outskirts of Tel Aviv." Then she phoned the Jaffa Hostel. They had one room left for forty dollars "You're lucky," she said "You'll like it there. You might even have an ocean view." Afterwards she showed me an ad in a booklet that said, "Our Jaffa Hostel offers you the most romantic, beautiful rooms in Tel Aviv." I hoped it was true!

After a long and complicated bus ride to Jaffa, I wasn't prepared for what I was about to experience: When I climbed into a taxi, it took me through the worst looking slums, I have ever seen: Narrow, dark streets were lined with dilapidated buildings, trash heaps were piled waist high and alley cats darted in and out. Without streetlights it looked like the perfect hangout for hooded gangsters . . . . Even though I thrive on adventure, this time I felt I had crossed over the line. Flirting with danger scared me to death.

We stopped in front of an old, rundown, three-story building. For fear of being mugged, I rang the bell as quickly as possible. The door creaked open. Inside, I discovered a dingy entrance where plaster was peeling off the unpainted walls and grimy, threadbare carpets covered the stairway. I tried not to freak out. I reminded myself that unpleasant situations sometimes turn out O.K—a "dime store" philosophy perhaps, but it usually helps. When I climbed up to the third floor, a pretty, young African receptionist greeted me. I felt better for a moment until I saw the room. It was so small it looked like a closet. There was no outside window, only a small opening onto a stuffy hallway.

"I can't stay here," I complained in a disturbed voice. She looked disappointed. "Well, you can always sleep outside on the roof."

From the expression on my face, she knew that was an unacceptable solution. Then she thought a moment. "If the people who reserved room 31 don't arrive by eleven, you can stay there."

I examined room 31. It looked shabby, but at least it had a fan, a window and a balcony. With a weary sigh, I threw my backpack in the corner and stepped into the hallway to wash my hands. Just then a nice looking man in his 40's walked by. "How do you stand this place?" I asked, wanting to share my disappointment. He smiled. "That's exactly what my wife said last night when we arrived. We made our reservations from Germany over the Internet, and by looking at their website we expected to find a romantic get-away." We both laughed. I liked his sense of humor. He told me that he came from Ireland and was teaching English near Frankfort. When I mentioned that I would like to get something to eat, he suggested going out to a *falafel* stand. "Come and meet my wife. Maybe she'd like to go with us."

Betty, who was from Uganda, was lying on the balcony too tired and hot to move, but Paul, their teenaged son, agreed to go. That night, after eating delicious *falafel* sandwiches, the three of us strolled along the beach, joking about our "romantic, ocean front rooms". By the time I returned to the hostel, my spirits had improved, especially after hearing that room 31 was mine!

PART 7

JAFFA, TEL AVIV, & JERUSALEM

Since I arrived at the Jaffa Hostel after midnight, I was looking forward to a long, peaceful sleep. But it didn't happen. About 5:00 am I heard motors roaring, brakes screeching, people shouting. "What the going on?" I barked, angrily. Half asleep, I staggered to the balcony to investigate. Below, from a jumble of trucks, vans and horse-drawn carts, I saw men busily unloading everything imaginable: shabby sofas, used refrigerators, old tires, whatever. Just my luck! I exclaimed, "A 'bloody' flea market underneath my window!"

The Jaffa Hostel in Isreal

Too upset to go back to sleep, I stomped down to the kitchen to cook my simple breakfast of cereal, toast and tea. Since the Jaffa Hostel was a run-down, scruffy place, I expected to see guests with long, matted haired and earrings in their nostrils. However, that wasn't the case. Those sharing the small, basic kitchen were all interesting travelers from every corner of the globe. I met an Austrian doctor working in Brazil, a young Australian on a Middle East tour and an Irish journalist doing odd jobs in Tel Aviv. Listening to their stories and travels was so fascinating; I hung around the dining room for the entire morning.

Around noon I decided to examine the bustling flea market. Weaving in and out of parked trucks and piles of junk, I found a narrow lane, choked with colorful carpet vendors and glistening brass dealers. Then, pushing my way through a covered, crowed musty smelling alleyway, I discovered an exotic bazaar. On one side sat clothes merchants snuggled under their garments that hung from the ceiling, and on the other side silversmiths squatted on platforms in front of their jewelry. After browsing a bit, I bargained for some silver looking, engraved bracelets. Pleased with the reduced price, I bought two.

Later, I wandered down to Jaffa's small harbor, supposedly founded by Noah's eldest son and one of the world's oldest. Being in operation for more than 4000 years, it attracted many conquerors on its shores: Phoenicians, Persians, Egyptians, and even courageous Napoleon. In spite of its a 'top-of-the-line' historical past, the port looked unimpressive. It did have a good view of Tel Aviv, though. In the distance I could see its wide, crescent bay rimmed by tall, luxury hotels. Like Rio De Janeiro, it boasted of being a metropolis with a beach.

On my second day in Jaffa, I caught a bus into Tel Aviv to the Egyptian Embassy. We passed dingy shops, a few open markets and pockets of modern buildings. It seemed to be a sprawling, unplanned city. Too bad the expensive hotels had grabbed up all the beachfront real estate. If the city had faced the lovely blue Mediterranean, it would have been a more attractive place.

I had to leave my passport at the Egyptian Embassy for three hours for a visa, so I wandered down to the beach. Acting like a well-to-do guest, (I combed my hair) I stepped into the Hilton's five-star, air-conditioned lounge, in order to avoid the oppressive heat. As I was enjoying the comfort of a plush sofa, some rich American tourists and their Israeli relatives sat down near me. I couldn't help overhearing their conversation.

"The first place I think you should visit is Jaffa," the Israeli lady said, planning her guests' sightseeing tour. "I'm sure you'll like its old world charm, especially the flea market."

Flea market! I chuckled to myself—never imagining my tacky hostel was overlooking a tourist attraction! In fact, the whole neighborhood around the Jaffa Hostel was so dingy and dirty, I thought I was staying on the wrong side of town!

After four days at the Jaffa Hostel, I left on an easy 50-minute bus ride to Jerusalem. Here I stayed inside the walled city of Old Jerusalem.

I loved its age-old ways. Every day I'd thread my way by foot through narrow, cobblestone alleys to one of the five religious quarters: In the Christian area, I saw the Church of the Holly Sepulchre, where Jesus was crucified and buried; in the Armenian part, I attended an orthodox catholic mass; and in the Temple Mount, a Muslim area, I visited the Dome of the Rock, an Islamic monument built around the stone where Abraham was willing to sacrifice his son.

The church in Jersusalem

Then, in the Jewish section I prayed at the women's side of the Western Wall, the only remains of their temple, destroyed by the Romans in 70 AD. Being a pragmatist, I couldn't understand why the Jews insisted on worshiping at a wall, instead of forgetting the past and building a new temple in their own quarter. The power of religious tradition, I suppose.

Frequently stories appeared in the newspaper revealing this rigidity. For example the orthodox Jews, the ones dressed in black, believe that no one should drive a car on the Sabbath. When the unorthodox Jews who disagree with their religious view and insist on driving near there, these traditionalists block the road and throw stones. Often the police have to interfere.

In Jerusalem it appears that the different Jewish Sects outside the walls have more difficulty living together than the various religious groups inside the Old City.

To visit Israel's other important sites, I took a couple day excursions. I saw Nazareth, the Sea of Galilee, the Jordan River, the Masada and the Dead Sea. Seeing how dry and barren Israel's landscape was—not even a bush or a weed growing in the desert soil—made me wonder how this bleak area could have ever been called the Promised Land.

One tour I missed altogether. I was planning to catch a 7:00 o'clock bus so I hurried down to the hostel lobby at 6:30 a.m. And guess what? The front door was locked, and no one was at the reception desk. In panic, I rang a buzzer on the counter, almost loud enough to wake up the dead. Yet no desk clerk appeared. Then I knocked on the doors of a few sleeping guests. Still no results. Realizing I was about to miss my bus, I woke up Andrea, a young American graduate student, sleeping on a couch in the hallway. She found a set of keys, but none fit. From all the commotion I made, a whole crew of sleepy guests gradually assembled in the lounge. While they were giving me suggestions—like using a fire escape that didn't exist—a young boy came down the stairs wearing his backpack.

"Where are you going?" we asked, chuckling.

"I'm leaving this place," he complained. "It's too noisy."

We apologized and told him to try again later when the door was unlocked. In disgust, he returned to his room.

When I realized that my hostage status was not going to change for a while, I began to relax. One guest, a minister from Singapore, made me a cup of coffee in the kitchen, and another whipped me up some breakfast. "This is the most community I have ever seen in this place." Andrea commented. She stayed here often while doing research for her thesis on the Palestinian plight.

Finally, about eight the mysterious desk clerk appeared; he had been comfortably sleeping in a vacant room upstairs. Upon seeing our gathering, his only remark was, "You should have told me you were leaving so early!"

To change my plans, that afternoon I joined Andrea on her field trip to a Palestinian settlement at Hebron. Together with a translator-guide, we took a *sherut* (shared taxi) through bleak hills to a refugee camp. First, we visited a family living in a simple concrete house, then walked through the dirt streets, followed by a string of cute, wide-eyed, barefooted children.

Later in a bare community room, we joined a meeting of the elders. Dressed like Arafat, with head coverings and long white gowns, they sat in a circle on the floor. For over an hour Andrea and I asked them questions about the Palestinian problem. They told us about losing their homes and land in the war and expressed bitterness about their poor living conditions. "We want equal rights with the Israeli's," they kept repeating. "Now we pay taxes and have no power." They also felt that Arafat was not doing enough for them.

Missing my bus that morning turned out better than I anticipated. It gave me the chance to visit a Palestinian settlement that I had always wanted to see.

PART 8

JERUSALEM TO CAIRO

CAIRO, EGYPT

Building in Cairo, Egypt

After Israel, my following destination was Tunisia. Since no planes flew directly from Tel Aviv, I had to leave from Egypt. The most exciting way to go, I thought, would be by bus through the historic Sinai Desert. This assumption, though, was wrong. The long journey was so unpleasant that riding a camel or "footing" it like Moses would have been better.

All along the way we had delays: The 7:00 o'clock Mazada bus from Jerusalem left an hour late. Then, we stopped in Tel Aviv just to collect the driver's eight-year-old daughter who came along for the ride.

This shy, little girl sat in the front seat next to me. Her father, a friendly man with two missing front teeth, told me he had seven other children.

"Why so many?" I inquired curiously.

"God gave them to me, and He'll take care of them," was his answer. Later, he boasted that he would soon take an additional wife. As a Muslim, he is allowed four.

I wondered if he thought the more children he had the richer he was! I know the Bedouins feel that way.

At our next stop, we picked up two stern-looking soldiers with machine guns. Stomping through the aisles, they inspected our documents. Every time they carried my passport off the bus, I prayed I wouldn't be accused of being a "sneaky" spy. In my travels, this had happened twice: once in Iraq and another time in Russia. Both were scary experiences I didn't wish to repeat.

Our passport examinations continued. I never knew if they were random road checks or the border formalities of Gaza Strip, where Arafat now resides.

Further down the road, we drove by a deserted area with so many rows of bob wire it looked like we were entering a war zone. After that, we continued to the Palestinian border near Rafah. Here we changed buses and drivers and had more passport checks. Those on the Egyptian side were the worst. A Palestinian couple in front of me stood in lines for three hours just to get through customs. An example of not trusting your neighbors, I guess.

Here, in the sweltering heat, we waited for hours. No one had a clue when we would leave. Before our driver went to sleep in the shade of his bus, I tried to ask him. Speaking only Arabic, he answered me by stretching his arms up and looking at the sky. I think he meant, "God only knows!"

Finally, about 2:30 our bus pulled out behind a string of five vans and four other buses. At that moment, I realized the reason of our delay: We were crossing the Sinai desert in a convoy. Two siren-screeching police cars escorted us, supposedly to scare off would-be attackers.

This convoy reminded me of the one I experienced in Africa in the 60's. Because of the Sudan's civil war, my Italian husband and I were forced to leave the village where we had been working. Accompanied by fifty army trucks, we spent two grueling, anxious days bumping along on rutted, dirt roads. Fortunately, we reach our destination safely. But in the convoy after ours, one man was shot and killed by the ambushing rebels. I hoped I'd arrive safely this time, too. To be a hostage, for some fund-raising terrorist event, didn't appeal to me.

The scenery through the Sinai desert was bleak, barren and boring. Only occasionally we passed a Bedouin mud hut and some goats. Few people live here because of the lack of water. The Egyptian government is trying to change this, though. They are building a narrow channel from the Suez Canal in hopes of transporting water. They are also offering free land to new settlers.

About six thirty, just as the sun was dipping below the horizon like an orange ball of fire, we arrived at the Suez Canal. A wide ribbon of water with sandy shores was all we saw, because the big ships had already passed by. Still, in the evening's balmy air, to ferry across the Suez Canal was exciting.

The nearer we got to Cairo, the more horrendous the traffic became. To go 12 km took over an hour. There seemed to be only two traffic rules: pass the car in front any way you can and constantly honk your horn. I wondered if they stopped pretending they were racecar drivers and stayed in one lane, would they all run into one another?

About ten thirty we finally arrived in the center of Cairo. Instead of pulling into a bus station, the bus driver dumped us off on the edge of a congested roundabout where cars whizzed around us.

To search for a hotel, I shared a taxi with a young Bulgarian doctor and his wife. We told our driver the address of a budget hotel, but he couldn't understand us. Finally, he gave up in frustration and let us off on a busy boulevard.

For over an hour, exhausted and hungry, we trudged from hotel to hotel, but all were full. Finally, we ended up at the dumpy Claridge Hotel on the 5th floor. Their rickety, cage-like elevator looked like a suicide trap, so we had to climb up the five flights of stairs, carrying our heavy backpacks.

Just like my trip, my room was the ultimate in discomfort. Not only was it dirty, hot and infested with buzzing mosquitoes, but it had only one small window that opened onto a courtyard below where a TV blasted away. Nevertheless, in spite of all this, I eventually drifted off to sleep.

My next day in Cairo was wonderful! I loved the city's pulsing life and historic sites. Having spent two months in the Middle East, I was used to its confusing ways and found Cairo less chaotic than on my previous trips.

Because my plane to Tunisia left the following day, I crammed all my sightseeing into 24 hours. First, I roamed through the noisy, bustling streets. Then, I sat down in a coffee house and watched men leisurely smoke their *Shishas* (water pipes with long hoses). A waiter lights the requested amount of tobacco and serves the pipe to his customers. Seeing the smokers' contented expressions, made me wish I were daring enough to smoke one, too.

Later, I taxied to Saludin Square in Old Islamic Cairo. Here, I gazed upon a cluster of beautiful medieval mosques that made me feel I had stepped back in time.

After entering several of them, I began my climb to the hilltop citadel, built by Saludin in 1176 to fortify the city against the crusaders. Unable to find the entrance, I sat down in a sidewalk café for a cup of mint tea. From an adjacent table, a man informed me, in French, that I was walking in the wrong direction. Being a kind soul, he drove me up the hill in his new Chinese-made truck used for delivering meat!

From this fortress, where Egypt's rulers lived for 700 years, a panorama of Cairo stretched below: tall, slender minarets rose above the houses and the slow moving Nile snaked through the city. The view was spectacular!

Inside the Citadel's sturdy walls stood many ancient monuments. The most impressive one was the huge, alabaster mosque and mausoleum built by Mohammed Ali in 1848. He was a famous warrior and ruler who successfully expelled the British from Egypt.

At closing time, I returned to the entrance where taxi drivers dove at me like seagulls fighting for a lone piece of bread. The one I selected spoke the best English and offered the best price.

As I sat down in his taxi, a poorly dressed vendor dumped a stack of colorful, Egyptian papyrus-scrolls onto my lap. Thinking they wouldn't fit in my backpack, I told him I wasn't interested. Still, he kept insisting and lowering his price. Unable to resist a good bargain, I finally bought three. Only a dollar a piece.

Suddenly out of nowhere, a plain-dressed man appeared on the scene. He grabbed the hawker by the neck and drug him away.

"What's going on?" I asked my driver.

"He's being arrested for harassing a tourist."

I felt sad. Maybe I was responsible.

As we approached Giza, the three enormous pyramids rose majestically from the desert floor. A calm, mystical feeling descended over me. I was glad I had a chance to see them again.

In the evening, after I ate a quick meal at a nearby Mac Donald's, I continued my sightseeing. The same taxi driver drove me to an ancient mosque, where men in long, colorful skirts spun and whirled to the melodies of high-pitched flutes. Watching Sufi dancing was a perfect way to end the day.

SECTION II
BACKPACKING IN AFRICA

Map of Africa

PART 1

CAPE TOWN AND VICINITY

July, First Week

As I stepped off the airport bus in Cape Town, Table Mountain loomed in the distance. I never imagined it would be such a spectacular backdrop for the entire city. I stood admiring it for awhile, then began looking for a bus to my hostel. When it never came, I finally climbed upstairs to a tourist office and asked for help. What's that?

Table Mountain in view from Cape Town

"It's a cheap taxi that you share." Noticing my backpack, she assumed I wasn't in the market for an expensive taxi—She was right, of course!

In front of a noisy bus station, I waited for the "rikki". When it pulled up along side the curb, to my surprise, it wasn't a car at all. It was an open pickup truck that had seen better days. And the driver was an elderly woman with gray, bobbed hair! Loving the novelty of all this, I climbed up in the back and plopped down on a wooden bench. As we whipped around corners, the spirited driver shouted, "We're going to pick up some more passengers."

"That's fine," I shouted back, not knowing in which direction I was really suppose to be going anyway. We darted in and out of Cape Town's narrow streets and at last pulled up in front of the Zebra Crossing Hostel.

"Here you are," she yelled over the traffic.

I rang the bell beside a locked gate, and Marius, the director, appeared, greeting me with a cordial smile. I had no idea if the hostel would be a suitable place for someone in her senior years, but his warm welcome put me at ease. The hostel turned out to be a charming place. It had dormitories, a community kitchen, a sitting room, two shady brick patios, and in front of the office bulletin boards advertising budget African tours.

Marius gave me a small, single room across from a cozy, warm café. Here I spent many hours, not only for meals but just trying to keep warm. July is wintertime in Cape Town and freezing cold!

The guests I met were fascinating. They came from all over the world and had fascinating stories to tell about their unusual adventures: One middle aged English couple had taken an overland truck tour for six months all the way down from North Africa.

Some Americans, on vacation from Peace Corps, were teaching in Malawi and Lesotho and three youthful Norwegians boys had just cycled down from Ethiopia. Africa's wildness seems to attract the most adventurous souls.

Harbor in Cape Town

After hearing so many fascinating tales, I immediately changed my whole itinerary. Instead of one month in Africa, I decided to spend three. Knowing that most things in life can be changed—that is, if you're willing to pay the price—I asked Marius to cancel all my flight and safari reservations. Literally, I wiped the board clean and started over again. In spite of the cost, this was a decision I never regretted.

My first trip from Cape Town was to the Cape of Good Hope. On a rainy, gray morning Day Tripper's touring van picked me up at the hostel. We drove south along a windy road that hugged steep cliffs jetting into the ocean. The dramatic coastline, with its deep indented bays, reminded me of the gorgeous scenery along Northern California's Highway One. When the narrow road straightened out, Craig, our guide and driver—so handsome he could melt any woman's heart, including mine—unloaded our bikes from the trailer behind our van. Then off we cycled to the cape, listening to the roaring waves of the Atlantic Ocean and occasionally braking for raucous baboons crossing the road. What a great experience!

At Cape Point, we climbed steep steps to view the lighthouse sitting on the very tip of a protruding rock. Here two oceans meet. On one side is the Indian Ocean and on the other the Atlantic. Most people think that Cape Point is the southern most tip of the African continent, but recent satellite pictures have revealed it's not true. The nearby Point Agulhas (needle in Portuguese) on the Indian Ocean side extends farther south.

After visiting Cape Point, we hopped on our bikes again and pedaled to the entrance of the Cape of Good Hope, now a large nature reserve. In 1487 the explorer, Bartholomew Dias, a Portuguese, was the first to sail around it. Because of its treacherous currents, and being a realist, he named it the Cape of Disaster. The Portuguese king, however, not wanting to discourage other daring explorers, renamed it, The Cape of Good Hope. Like Columbus, Diaz was on his way to India for spices.

My next trip with Day Trippers Tours was a visit to a black township outside of Cape Town. Officially called an informal settlement, it was actually a shanty town filled with squatter shacks built of wood, corrugated sheets or cardboard. Though depressing, it was necessary to see in order to understand South Africa's history and segregation. Until 1995, the blacks were forced to live here. In fact, they weren't allowed to be in Cape Town after six p.m.—otherwise they would be arrested.

In the township, we sat inside a "shabeen", a shed used as a bar or meeting place. Here we listened to men tell about their lives during apartheid. The stories were grim. Without their families, the men were shipped here from their villages to work as laborers in mines and construction. If a man's wife wanted to visit him from the countryside, she needed to obtain a special permit. What's worse, every black and colored person (people of mixed blood) had to always carry an identification card. Thank goodness with the new government these rules have changed.

The second part of our tour couldn't have been more pleasant. We visited wineries in Stellenbosch, where we sipped wine to our hearts content. Nestled among high, imposing mountains sits the wine district, a lush valley of rows and rows of vineyards, even more beautiful than Napa Valley.

Many of the wineries were started by the French Huguenots who came here in the 17th century, seeking religious freedom like our pilgrims. In France the Catholics persecuted them because they had become Calvinists (Protestants).

The wine we sampled was excellent—as well as dirt-cheap. Imagine buying a good bottle of wine for only three dollars! Since the American dollar was worth six rand, everything in South Africa seemed like a bargain.

Before leaving the wine district, we passed the prison where President Mandela spent the last three years of his 27 years in prison. When he was released in 1990, no one ever thought his life term would ever be rescinded and that he would one day become President. One of history's great surprises!

PART 2

CAPE TOWN

July, First Week

Today was another cold, rainy day in Cape Town. Perfect weather, I thought, for exploring museums. Bundled up in wool sweaters, like on a ski slope, I strolled to the Cultural History Museum. It was a historical building, originally built in 1679 as a slave lodge for the Dutch East Indian Company. Who'd think that they would need to import slaves into Africa! But the natives on the Cape refused to work for the Dutch. Being hunters, all they wanted to do was steal their cattle! Consequently, the colonists brought in slaves from Malaysia, Indonesia and Madagascar. Today, these brown skinned people make up part of South Africa's colored race.

The museum showed exhibits from the Dutch and English colonial period. The "postal stones" from along the coast were the most interesting. They were engraved with the names of passing ships indicating caches of letters left by the crews. The senders hoped that their letters would be picked up by the next ship heading in the right direction. A system about as efficient as Africa's current postal service. Two months for a Cape Town postcard to reach France is a bit long, don't you think?

The second museum I visitedthat day was the South African Museum, a perfect place to learn about Africa's history: The first inhabitants (after the stone-age tribes) were the San, known as Bushmen. A short, brown skinned nomadic people, they lived off the land, eating plants and killing wild animals with bows and poison arrows. Perhaps not a bad way to live, if the weather held out!

Related to the San were the Khoikhoi (Hottentots), who were semi-nomadic sheep and cattle herders. Together, these two groups are referred to as the Khoisan. Unfortunately, like our Indians, they were eventually driven from their lands and tragically killed by the white man's diseases or superior weapons. Today, only a few still exist in Botswana and Nambia. Because of their primitive "lifestyle"—wearing no clothes, for instance—they are a frequent stop on the tourist circuit!

The third racial group to arrive on the scene (about the eleventh century) were the Bantu speaking tribes. They settled in the northern and eastern part of the country and were black. More advanced than the Khoisan, they knew how to make iron tools, domesticate animals, plant farm crops and live in villages.

These different races, together with the Dutch, English, French, German and Indians, compose South Africa's varied population. That's why it's known as "the rainbow nation." Similar to Americans, most of the six million white South Africans have a mixture of European ancestors.

On my second rainy day, I visited the mall at the Victoria Alfred Waterfront. Here I realize that part of South Africa is as developed as the States. Resembling Costa Mesa's South Coast Plaza, it was huge with beautiful shops and restaurants. Many of the sales people were attractive women with bronze colored skin, big black eyes and lovely faces. Curious, I asked an especially gorgeous one what her background was. Her answer surprised me. "I'm colored (mixed races)," she replied proudly. In the mall, I also noticed that there were only a few blacks, probably because they don't have enough money to shop here.

After four days of bad weather, a few rays of sunshine pierced the gray clouds that hung over Table Mountain, called the "table cloth" by the locals. When I saw the clear blue sky, I immediately jumped in a "Rikki" (cheap taxi) and headed for the cableway that had been closed for a few days.

As I stood in a long line waiting to buy my ticket for the summit, I had my first conversation with a black South African, a middle aged man standing with his family. He told me he had graduated from a university in the States and now organized schools and teacher training for the black townships outside of Cape Town. He seemed optimistic about South Africa's future, something most white South Africans don't feel. With the new black South African government, they think that the country is deteriorating.

On top of Table Mountain, 3000 ft. high, the views were phenomenal. Bathed in the afternoon sunlight, the silent blue sea stretched along an enormous crescent shaped bay. Tall buildings stood beside its shores and red roofed cottages clung to the hillside below. A view so spectacular, it was easy to understand why Cape Town is considered one of the world's most beautiful cities.

As I climbed over the craggy rocks and walked along the dirt paths, more exhilarating views assaulted me. On my left—along the rugged shoreline—tiny, picturesque coves lay hidden below the steep cliffs. Then to the back of Table Mountain, steep dramatic gorges extended down to the green carpeted valley below. Seeing this beauty, I felt grateful that my wish to see Cape Town had finally come true.

Though I hated leaving the Zebra Crossing Hostel, I finally decided it was time to see more of the country.

The Zebra crossing Hostel

Marius, the friendly hostel director, arranged my reservations on the Baz Bus, a fantastic service for backpackers. For only about a hundred dollars, the bus would take me all around South Africa. Not only that, I could hop off and on as many times as I wanted. The bus would drop me off on the steps of any hostel on my list and pick me up when I was ready to leave. How can you beat that!

First, I planned to travel along the Garden Route, then visit Durban, the Drakenberg Mountains and eventually end up in Johanesberg.

PART 3

GARDEN ROUTE—AN AREA OF SCENIC BEACHES, MOUNTAINS, RIVERS AND FORESTS.

July, Second Week

In the early morning mist, the Baz tour bus picked me up at Zebra Crossing Hostel, headed for the Garden Route. The friendly, colored driver loaded my pack back into the trailer behind the bus, then drove to the other hostels for more passengers.

On the outskirts of Cape Town we eased onto the freeway. I never expected to find such a beautiful four-lane highway with <u>no traffic</u>! When I lived in Africa before in the sixties, all we had outside of Khartoum (Sudan) were narrow, bumpy, dirt tracks. Not even roads!

My seat companion on the bus was Patrick, an Irish lad with a great sense of humor. When he introduced me to his traveling buddy from London, he joked, "See, the English and Irish, <u>can</u> get along."

For six months they had been sightseeing in southern Africa and told me the places to visit. "Don't miss Namibia," he emphasized. "You'll love the pink sand dunes! They're spectacular!" With his recommendation, I added one more country to my long list.

Our first stop that morning was for breakfast and gas. At a filling station, all of us piled out of the bus and hurried over to a nearby strip-mal. For the weary traveler, it had everything: a grocery store, restaurant, souvenir shop and enormous white-tiled rest rooms with a full-time black attendant. This mall was also a rest stop for the huge Intercape and Translux buses. These luxurious, double-deckers travel to most of the main cities. After seeing such modern facilities, I understood why South Africa's is often called the "United States of Africa".

Farther down the road we stopped again. This time to let off passengers at Mossel Bay, known for mussels and whale watching. When I saw the unique hostel on the beach, I wished I were staying there, too. It was located inside train carriages stationed right along a horseshoe-shaped bay that stretched as far as you could see.

By afternoon we reached Wilderness, a sleepy resort, perfectly situated beside a river, beach and mountains. Here I stayed at the Fairy Knowe hostel. With its long veranda across the front, it resembled a typical African lodge. All the dorms and double rooms were located in an old wooden house at the end of a winding path through the bush. From my corner, upstairs room, I gazed upon pine-covered mountains on one side and a slow, meandering river on the other. With these magnificent views, I wanted to stay here forever.

Shortly after my arrival in Wilderness, I had a very scary experience. As the afternoon light began to fade, I was strolling back to the hostel, after a long walk to the beach and village market. Since I feared I might be late for dinner, I turned off the main street to a deserted road that I thought might be a short cut. Shortly, though, when the sun dipped below the horizon, the sky became pitch black. With no twilight, no street lamps, no star-lit sky, I was immediately engulfed in a blanket of darkness.

Many times I had been warned <u>not to be out alone at night.</u> And here I was all by myself.

Frightened that I might be mugged, I quickly concealed my expensive Nikon camera underneath my jacket. Then I hid the 1200 rand (about 200$) that I had just drawn out at the ATM inside my bra. The safest place I could think of.

But as I continued down the road, I had another misfortune. The road ended in a dead end, and I was totally lost!

"Nothing to do but turn around," I said to myself, feeling angry that my adventurous spirit had betrayed me. Hurrying through the dark, I suddenly heard three African ladies singing. At first, I wanted to hide for fear of being robbed. But after a quick and anxious dialogue with myself, I decided to ask for help.

"Excuse me," I said cautiously, "Could you direct me to Fairy Knowe, please?"

They looked at one another, then one finally spoke. "Follow us," she said. Then they led me down a bumpy dirt path, through a spooky forest and along a deserted railroad track

One of the women spoke a little English. She told me that they worked as maids in a nearby hotel and came from a distant Xhosa village. Since their husbands couldn't find jobs, they had to leave their families and children to come here. Unfortunately, in South Africa unemployment is terribly high. Out of a population of 44 million about 50% are without work.

After a half-hour—which seemed much longer—we reached the hostel. Relieved that my nightmare was over, I gave each woman a few rand for delivering me safe and sound.

After dinner that night all of us guests sat around a big open bonfire and told stories. The owner, a lean, rugged looking Welshman, had the most interesting one.

He told us how he happened to come to Africa.

"In my twenties, I traveled all the way down the African continent on my motorcycle," he said proudly. "But in South Africa I stayed too long and my visa expired so the government sent me back to Wales.

"Later, I applied for a job to come back and found one on a demolition squad. One day, while I was blowing up a building in Johanesberg, I noticed a beautiful lady in the crowd watching us." He paused for a moment, as if reflecting on that special occasion. "Then, by chance, I met her again at a party. She was an Afrikaner (Dutch origin) and born here. In about a year we got married and moved to Wilderness. I love it here," he said, poking the fire with a stick. "I never want to live anywhere else."

After three days at Fairy Knowe, I left on an old steam train that ran in front of the hostel. To catch the train, I stood alone by the railroad tracks and waved to the engineer. When he saw me, he waved back and blew his whistle. Then, just for me, he stopped the whole train. I felt like a celebrity!

The train chugged along at a snail's pace, and the windows rattled, the cars swayed, the engine hissed. All us passengers seemed pleased with our fantasy-like experience. We smiled at one another, as if to say, "Isn't this great fun?"

We passed lakes, forests, rivers and beaches. Our end station was Krysna, a town that faced an immense lagoon with a river on the side. Except for a narrow opening into the ocean, the lagoon was completely surrounded by tall, red sandstone cliffs. It was gorgeous.

At Krysna, the Baz Bus met me and off I went farther down the Garden Route.

PART 4

GARDEN ROUTE: PLETTENBERG BAY AND NATURES VALLEY

July, Second Week

My next stop on the Garden Route was at a trendy resort called Plettenberg Bay. Beautifully situated on a hill, it overlooked white sand beaches, a clear blue lagoon and hazy distant mountains. After seeing its elegant shops and hotels, I understood why it was a white man's playground.

The Kurlands Hostel

In fact, with no black people on the streets, it was hard to believe I was in Africa. When I finally saw an African vendor, dressed in a long skirt and head scarf, I asked if I could take her picture. Obligingly, she posed for me, probably wondering why I selected her to photograph.

One of my favorite past times in Plettenberg Bay was sitting in restaurants, eating fresh fish. The coziest pub in town, and with the best ocean view, was the Crown and Anchor. While munching at the bar on crunchy fried *calamari* (squid), I chatted with the local fishermen

Bob, a big, rugged-looking man in his forties, told me all about fishing. "It's a hard life," he said as he slurped his rum and coke. "But I love the ocean and don't think I could ever do anything else."

Later he added, "We go out for about five days at a time. If we bring the frozen fish back in less than a week, we can sell it as fresh fish."

Hmmm . . . . interesting! In my innocent world, I thought fish had to wiggle to be fresh.

My other past time at Plettenberg Bay was strolling along its quiet, empty beaches. I liked watching the young surfers ride the waves and the men get their loaded dinghies through the wild surf. Before they could start their engines and motor out to the fishing boats off shore, they had get beyond the breakers. Not an easy job from what I observed.

My hostel at Plettenberg Bay was nothing special, just an ordinary house in a residential area. To convert it into a hostel, its owners had filled the bedrooms with bunk beds. Since they lived next door, in their fancy bed and breakfast, we backpackers had the whole house to ourselves. Not bad!

I prefer staying in hostels, instead of hotels, for several reasons. First, the price fits my skimpy budget: a double room costs about $15, a dorm $7. Second, I can whip up something in the kitchen if I want. And third, there is always someone around to talk to.

Even though I'm always the oldest backpacker—in the senior citizen category—it never bothers me. That is, as long as no one tries to make me the "house mother"!

After two days in Plettenberg Bay's warm sunshine, the Baz Bus picked me up and delivered me down the road to Natures Valley. Originally, I had planned to stay by the beach, but when I saw Kurland Backpacker's Farm I changed my mind.

It was absolutely beautiful! Just like in expensive hotels, tall, stately cypress trees lined the private road that led to the entrance. My room was in one of the whitewashed bungalows bordering the main lodge. From my veranda, I could gaze upon a huge lawn dotted with all kinds of trees and wild scrubs. It was a thrill to stay in such attractive surroundings.

The young owner, Peter, was a handsome man with a kind heart as well as a charming personality. He had graduated from a university in the States and only recently converted his family farm into a backpacker's hostel. Before that, he ran a business with his brother in Johannesburg. They imported used clothing from the States and sold it to the Africans.

Kurland Farm had a fascinating history. Originally it belonged to Peter's grandfather, a Russian Baron. He grew up on a large estate surrounded by pine forests, that was located in Kurland province in one of Russia's Baltic States. When he emigrated to South Africa, probably for political reasons, he lived in Johannesburg where he met and married a wealthy Afrikaner. In the early 1940's, they bought this farm in Natures Valley. To emulate his estate in Russia, he planted over one million pine trees on the surrounding hills. Presently, Peter's father runs a sawmill across the road.

One evening, Liz, the New Zealand hostel manager and cook, invited us to a *brai* (barbecue). We all piled into the back of a pick up truck to Monkeyland. This was a new tourist attraction. The owner had recently sold his private game park up north—imagine being so rich—and invested in monkeys!

Yes, monkeys! Eighty of the them to be exact.

These little creatures roamed freely around the surrounding forest. But amazingly most were not from Africa. They were imported monkeys! Out of the eight different species in Monkeyland, only two spieces were from Africa. Why? My guide had a fascinating answer: it changed a monkey's behavior to live in a small forest: If they weren't of different species, they would inner breed. Out in the wild, this phenomenon doesn't take place. It only happens in captivity. See what stress can do! It even affects the animal kingdom!

The guests at the *brai* were friendly people, all white South Africans who lived in Natures Valley. Most were teachers, B&B owners, lettuce growers, contractors and dairy farmers. It amazed me how much we had in common even though we were from two different continents.

The part of the *brai* I didn't like was all the heavy drinking. We arrived about six in the evening but weren't served dinner until ten. With no snacks, no chips, not even a sliver of *butong* (beef jerky), I became famished, woozy and weak. Finally, in desperation, I volunteered to help cook the meat—hoping, of course, to secretly snatch a few succulent pieces. But no luck! Barbecuing was a man's domain.

After four hours of "boozing", you can imagine how much sense our conversations made. One portly gentleman introduced himself to me three times. I guess I wasn't too coherent either. I kept forgetting his name as well.

In retrospect, I wonder why these people liked to drink so much. It seemed to me they were living in paradise!

PART 5

PORT ELIZABETH & CINTSA

July, Third week

After two weeks on the Garden Route, I arrived in Port Elizabeth, a town rich with many old buildings of Edwardian and Victorian architecture. Today, however, it no longer reflects its former elegance. Neglected historical buildings, shabby streets and a run-down port make it an ugly city. Even the bustling downtown area with an exotic, African pulse is a place too dangerous to explore.

BUCANEERS BOOZE CRUISE

The Buccaneers Booze Cruise

In Port Elizabeth I stayed for two nights. Not for sightseeing, though, but for shopping. The shutter on my Nikon broke, so I had to buy a new camera. I also wanted to replace my Adidas with a pair of sturdy leather boots for trekking.

The hostel I selected was in the "white" suburbs outside of town. Around the corner were many reminders of home: theaters with the latest American movies, a Kentucky Fried Chicken, a Wendy's and even an imitation Seven Eleven. Western culture, if you can call it that, was not what I preferred to see in Africa, but at least everyone said it was a safe neighborhood at night. It turned out they were right. I did survive an "evening out" at Speedy's Pizza Parlor.

The morning I went shopping, I took a bus. In the cool, brisk, invigorating air, I stood on the street. A parade of mini-bus taxis passed in front of me, stopping, loading up and speeding off. Shortly, all the Africans around me had disappeared.

Since no bus was in sight, I asked a young man standing nearby if he thought it would be all right for me to take one of the mini-bus-taxis.

"I wouldn't." he answered, seriously. "It's not safe."

"Why's that?

"Too many accidents. They're always overcrowded and go too fast."

"Darn," I complained, disappointed that I couldn't participate in a local custom. It disturbed me, too, that I had to squelch my "go-native-desire".

Thinking that I had detected an American accent, I asked him if he was from the States.

"No, I'm from Canada," he replied, "but I've lived in L.A. I went to UCLA." Named Dustin, he worked as a zoologist for a game reserve.

When he realized that I "didn't have a clue" how to get to the mall, he offered to accompany me. "It's my day off," he said, keeping his eye out for the bus, "so I've got lots of time."

Without hesitation, I accepted his kind offer. And what a great help! Not only did he know his way around the huge, spread-out mall, but he was also an excellent bargainer.

I liked his wild animal stories, too. He told me his last job was transporting elephants to the nearby Addo Elephant Reserve. He brought them from Kruger Park to eliminate their surplus. Since elephants have no predators like other animals (except, of course, for illegal poachers), their population isn't easy to control.

"It was a difficult trip," he explained. "We had to keep turning the sedated elephants from side to side, because if they lie in one position too long, they break their ribs."

Imagine turning over a sleeping elephant—in a truck, no less!

Dustin also shared with me his concern about the future. Since South Africa has affirmative action, the white people feel they are discriminated against. "I hope I'll be able to continue working here," he added. "I've been here for ten years and would hate to leave." When we parted, I promised to send him a copy of my book, *Asian Adventure*, and he agreed to send me more animal stories. I hope he doesn't forget.

CInsta (north of Port Elizabeth)

Everyone I met raved about Buccaneers Backpacker's Lodge in Cintsa, and when I arrived, I immediately understood why. It was a fantastic place with a breathtaking view! The main lodge sat on a hill and faced a wide, sweeping blue lagoon and miles of unspoiled beaches. The people who owned the lodge were special, too. Not only were they friendly and hospitable, but they even planned afternoon activities for us everyday. My favorite one was the booze cruise down the river.

At Buccaneers, I had a rustic beach cottage with an ocean view. Since it had two bedrooms, I shared it—not my bedroom—with other backpackers.

Here, I met the most unusual person of my whole trip. His name was Yasek, and he came from Poland. No matter what he said or did, it surprised me.

For instance, when I entered the cottage for the first time, he was in the kitchen heating a metal rod on the stove. After it got red hot, he poked it inside a thick, four feet piece of bamboo.

"What are you doing that for?" I asked curiously.

Staring at me with his penetrating blue eyes, he explained that he was making an African musical instrument.

It didn't look like any instrument I've ever seen, so I continued watching him. Then came my next surprise: He told me that he hadn't come to South Africa for a safari or traveling, but to attend a three week Zen retreat. "While we were there, we couldn't talk the whole time" he said in his heavily accented English, "and we started meditating at three A.M." Personally, I could think of a better time to work on "spiritual repair", couldn't you?

The surprises continued. After the retreat he went to the Grahamstown Dance Festival. And what did he do there? He sold plastic, Japanese toy spiders to the spectators! "I made enough to pay for the whole trip," he said proudly. "They loved them!"

Wanting to know more about him, I asked him one day what he did in Poland. Another surprise! Besides being a musician and hawker, he also sold Rainbow vacuum cleaners and, believe it or not, Amway products.

Yasek's girl friend was traveling with him. She was a dentist from Germany whom he met at a Zen Conference in Warsaw. (A unique couple, wouldn't you agree?) Every night he cooked dinner for her and always invited me to join them. His potato pancakes and dumplings made a sumptuous feast!

Yasek, will always remain in my memories. He was truly a free spirit.

PART 6

COFFEE BAY, SOUTH OF DURBAN

Third Week

Out in the middle of nowhere, at an isolated filling station, the Baz bus dropped me off. "This is the Wild Coast stop," the driver called back at me. With only brown fields around, I hesitantly climbed down from the bus. Before I could panic about being stuck out here alone, a tired looking pick up truck pulled up beside me.

"Hi. Coffee Bay?" the young driver yelled. "Yeah," I shouted, happy to be rescued from "no man's land." I threw my backpack in the bed of his truck and climbed into the cab. "My name is Patrick," he said, with an Australian accent. From his long hair and bare feet, I sensed he was a "laid-back" kind of guy.

For two hours, we drove on narrow paved roads through the rolling, barren hills of the Transkei, a predominately African area where President Mandela was born. Turquoise painted rondavels (round huts) were scattered across the treeless landscape. For once, I felt I was really in Africa.

Finally, we pulled into the dusty village of Coffee Bay. Patrick parked his truck on the bank of what-looked-liked-a-river (actually an inlet from the ocean) and said nonchalantly, "The hostel is over there on the other bank. We'll have to wade across."

You gotta be kidding, I wanted to exclaim, but instead inquired politely, "Is this the usual procedure?"

TRANSKEI

The Transkei

"No, tomorrow, when the tide's low, I can drive across."

Cautiously, with boots off, pant legs rolled up and backpack slung across my shoulders I stepped into the deep water. While trying to avoid the slippery, sharp rocks, I wondered if anyone around here had ever heard of a bridge!

The hostel stood among palm trees directly behind another house that faced the ocean. Since the double room had no electricity, Patrick showed me to a dorm. Then he announced he had to open the bar. "Come over later, the first drink is on the house."

After unpacking a few things, I went over for a "free beer". Hardly bigger than a large closet, the bamboo-decorated bar was crowded with interesting people. Among the guests were the hostel owner, a wiry-looking fisherman; the elderly man from the front house who once had employed Africans for the mines in Johannesburg; a pretty veterinarian student from Slovenia (in love with the hostel owner); and an anthropology professor on a dig. His cute, young assistant accompanied him (probably also in love). Africa, it appears, attracts only romantic and adventurous souls.

Stayed only one night at Coffee Bay Backpackers. The next morning Patrick—after rescuing his truck from the other side of the river—drove me out to another hostel called White Clay. It sat on a hill overlooking a cozy cove encircled by jagged cliffs. Waves slapped against its pebbled beach, and African huts dotted the hills behind. Quiet, picturesque, isolated, it was just the place I had dreamed of finding

One morning, about noon, I was sitting on a wooden bench in front of my room listening to the roaring waves and admiring the surrounding beauty. Suddenly, a small barefoot African boy appeared before me. "You buy lobster?" he asked, holding the wiggling creature in his hand.

"How much?"

"Ten rand." (About 2$)

"OK", I said, glad to have a bargain. Grabbing it by the tail, I headed for our community kitchen. Just as I was about to throw the lobster into a pot of boiling water, another hostel guest entered.

"What are you doing with my lobster?" she exclaimed angrily.

"Your lobster?" I snapped back. "I just bought it for 10 rand.

"Well, it's mine. I paid 5 rand. I told a little boy to bring it up to the kitchen for me."

Not wanting to argue about the lobster's ownership, I relinquished my claim and ate my usual cheese sandwich for lunch.

But the lobster saga took an unusual turn.

Since it was a sunny day with teal blue skies and white floating clouds, I decided to walk to Hole in the Wall—an unusual rock about three hours away. Other hostlers had been there. Not reporting any messy encounter with danger, I assumed it was safe to walk there alone.

I climbed up a steep hill and followed the rugged coastline. After awhile, a narrow trail threaded through clusters of huts, where I met an African girl, balancing a bag of groceries on her head. She strolled leisurely along as stately and erect as a queen. Since I wasn't quite sure of the path, I asked her the way. She didn't speak English, but motioned for me to follow her.

We passed African women squatting in front of their mud huts, children with sparkling black eyes playing in the dirt and women climbing up from the beach holding baskets of mussels on top of their heads, gathered from the rocks below. Never have I walked so slowly in my life!

When the girl reached her rondavel, she motioned for me to continue straight ahead. I walked for another half an hour and came to a group of buildings. To my surprise, they turned out to be a first class hotel. Being curious, I peered into an open window and saw at an elegant dining room. Even though it was after three o'clock, two elderly men were sitting at a table eating lunch. In front of them sat a bottle of white wine and a large platter of lobster. "Hello," one of the men said, flashing me a warm smile.

"Hi," I answered, weary from my long hike.

"Would you like to join us?" he asked.

"I'd love to." And without hesitating, I walked inside and sat down. The waiter poured me a glass of wine and filled my plate with a delicious lobster. It was unbelievable! Fate must have been eavesdropping on my desires.

One of the men, Steve, was particularly charming. He had the air of someone used to living in the lap of luxury. He told me once owned a cold storage business in Durban. Now he was here on a fishing trip.

While we were dining together, the hotel manager joined us. She was a woman of cut diamond elegance, named Rose. The way Steve held her hand, and looked amorously into her eyes, meant that they, too, were deeply in love.

Later on, Rose asked a young boy to guide me to Hole in the Wall. Together we walked through forests, over boulders, along beaches and finally came to an immense rock, sitting in the ocean. The pounding of the waves had eroded a huge hole in the middle. It was, indeed, an impressive sight.

When I returned to the hotel, Rose called a truck-taxi to drive me back to the White Clay Hostel. The driver was another unusual man. Tall, thin, and about 45, he had worked all over Southern Africa, diving for diamonds in the rivers of the Central African Republic and off the coast of Angola. His stories entertained me all the way back.

What fun adventures, I had that day!

PART 7

DRAKENSBERG MOUNTAINS

Lesotho

Everyone I met insisted I see the Drakensberg (Dragon) Mountains. So, giving up my idyllic lifestyle at White Clay's beach side hostel, I reluctantly became a serious backpacker again.

My journey started on a crisp, sun-drenched morning. Patrick, the manager of the Coffee Bay hostel, came and picked me up. For two hours, we jostled along in his rickety, old truck to an "out-in-nowhere" filling station in Umtata. There I waited. When the Baz Bus arrived, it transported me down the road to Kokstad, three hours away. There I waited again. This time for a shuttle to Himeville, a small, predominately African town on the edge of the mountains.

The driver, a white South African, was an attractive, refined woman in her forties—not the type you'd expect to be driving a taxi. Named Jane, she ran the taxi business with her husband who insisted on living in Himeville so he could go fishing!

As we drove along on a two-lane country road, daylight gradually seeped from the sky, and evening shadows spread slowly across the vacant landscape.

"Aren't you afraid to be driving on these lonely roads?" I asked, noticing she showed no sense of fear.

"No, I have a cell phone," she replied nonchalantly, as if that would protect us from danger. Jane had grown up on a farm in the African bush and was probably accustomed to being the only car on the road.

After a long ride, I landed in front of the Himeville hotel. Here I waited once again. This time for a 4-wheel drive to take me up the mountains. When a jeep finally arrived, the driver was a bearded man named Russell, the hostel owner. I piled into his vehicle with other backpackers and jounced along on a gravel road.

By the time we reached the Sani Pass lodge, I was freezing and tired and famished. I was expecting to be revived by a hot, delicious meal but quickly learned that dinner was over at eight. In my grumpy mood, I made a cheese sandwich and wished I hadn't listened to the guy who told me the lodge served meals at any time.

The next morning, when I saw the magnificent, copper-colored mountains I felt better.

Unlike our towering California Sierras, whose gray rocky peaks jet into the sky, the Drakensbergs have low, flat summits or rounded ones like a camel's hump. Throughout the day they change their color. When the sun shines, the mountains have a fiery orange glow, and as the evening shadows creep over their craggy faces, they become a reddish brown. Their changing moods fascinated me.

While at Sani Pass Lodge, I joined one of Russell's hiking tours to see the famous San (Bushman) rock drawings. First, we threaded our way through forests, hills, steams and valleys, passing breathtaking scenery. Then, we climbed up the side of a mountain to a shallow cave. San paintings decorated the inside walls of the overhang. They were simple stick-figure-like drawings of people and animals, painted in red and depicting hunting scenes. It's amazing that this rock art, according to research, has existed here for over 250 years.

The San people came to the Drakensbergs in the summer time. They were astute hunters, using arrows with poisoned tips that came off and lodged inside the animal's skin. When it died later, they knew exactly how to track it down. Too bad these awesome hunters are now extinct in South Africa. Either they were killed in battle or intermarried with other African tribes.

LESOTHO

My second tour from the Sani Pass lodge was with four other guests to a tiny, mountainous country, called Lesotho. It has two million inhabitants and is completely surrounded by South Africa.

Lesotho at the Sani Pass

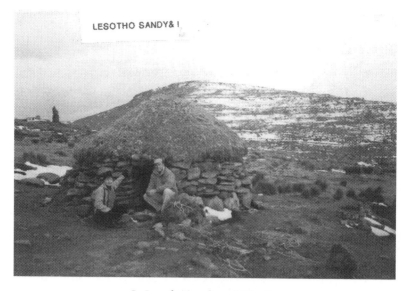

LESOTHO SANDY& I

In Lesotho Sandy and Martha

It was formed by a clever warrior, named Moshoeshoe. Originally, he was the headman of a Sotho village. In the 19th century, during the many gruesome Boer and Zulu wars, he accepted the destitute refugees into his tribe, thus increasing its size. Later, he brought his people to these mountains and named his kingdom Basutoland. Since his warring neighbors kept attacking his country, he asked the British for assistance. They agreed to help by annexing his land and eventually it became a British protectorate. In 1966, when the country gained its independence, the king renamed it Lesotho. Today many Peace Corps volunteers are working there. The ones I met love it.

It was a cloudy, rainy day when I left on the tour. Our guide, a-John-Wayne-type of man, was tall and sturdy with a zest for adventure. His name was Sandy, but I called him "the mountain man".

As he drove us through the steep Sani Pass on a pot-holed dirt road, he swished us around the mountain, like a racecar driver trying to finish first. The closer he drove to the cliff's edge, the happier he seemed to be. He scared us to death. Fortunately, a thick fog robed the mountain, so we couldn't see how far we'd fall, if he missed a hairpin curve.

At the Lesotho border, we stopped at the customs office to get our passports stamped. After that, we climbed to an elevation of 9000 feet. There at the summit, sat a rustic, isolated lodge, known to have the highest licensed pub in Southern Africa.

Upon arriving, we quickly ran inside to escape the bitter cold. Snuggled beside a crackling fire, we guzzled down steaming hot coffee to try and get warm. Carpeted and cozy, the lodge faced a barren, treeless landscape of alien starkness. It was the perfect place for someone who wanted to "get away from it all" and pretend they were on the moon.

Sandy, being a "mountain man", wouldn't let us be warm and comfortable for long. He insisted we continue our tour. First, he drove us to the top of a hill, where we could gaze upon the distant mountain peaks dusted with snow. Later, we investigated the interior of a deserted rondavel—a round hut made of stones (instead of mud) and covered with a thatched roof. In the summer time it's a sheepherder's refuge.

Our last stop was at a rondavel where a white flag was flying. This meant that freshly brewed beer was for sale. Wrapped in blankets, people were sitting inside on the floor around an open fire of cow dung. Sandy insisted we joined them for a real "native experience". But we didn't stay long. The smoke inside was thicker than L.A. smog. Before long our eyes began to water and our throats choked up. In order stop our coughing and breathe again, we all escaped. How these people can survive in these austere conditions is amazing.

On our way home, Sandy explained that sometimes the summit has heavy, unpredictable snowstorms. Once, he said, a professor was up there doing research and got caught unprepared in one of the unusual storms. A helicopter rescued him. After the snow melted, he returned to get his jeep. And guess what? He couldn't find it. The inhabitants had completely dismantled it and stolen the parts. All that was left of his jeep was the windshield!

PART 8

DURBAN & ESCHOWE (ZULULAND)

August (fifth week)

Arriving in Durban from the Drakensberg Mountains was like landing in the middle of New York City from the Ozarks. I felt overwhelmed by the imposing skyscrapers, the bumper to bumper traffic, the crowds of people. When I got used to the change, though, the city's beauty and vitality captivated me.

Market in Durban, South Africa

Durban seemed to have everything: ornate Victorian buildings, a bustlng port, elegant malls and a Miami-like ocean promenade flanked with luxury hotels. It even had a surfer's beach right in the middle of town and plenty of street markets and sidewalk vendors for African flavor.

Sundays were my favorite time. Flea markets popped up everywhere in Durban, and an air of festivity hung in the air. The best market, I found, was sandwiched between the Holiday Inn and the ocean promenade. In its rows and rows of stalls, vendors sold everything from: African woodcarvings, Zulu beaded bracelets, used books, clothes, kitchen utensils to whatever you could imagine. One man, I remember, displayed mainly safety pins. In fact, I felt sorry for him and bought some.

When I became weary of souvenir shopping, I wandered over to the food stalls. Enticed by the tangy scent of spices, I bought some curry and rice and somosas.

Then in the warm sunshine (It's summer all year round in Durban) I sat down at an empty table facing a band that was blasting out lively tunes.

Shortly, a pretty teenager joined me. From her bronze colored skin and frizzy hair, she didn't look Indian and nor African. Unable to squelch by curiosity, I tactfully asked where she was from.

She paused a minute, swallowing a mouth full of French fries. "I'm from Durban," she said with a half smile, not bothered by my question. Later she told me that she was colored (mixed races) and appeared to be proud of it. Over 3 ½ million colored people live in South Africa.

Before long, her father joined us. He had the same golden brown complexion but looked more African than his daughter.

While he waited for his wife to get off work from the Holiday Inn, we chatted about his family and job as a house painter. I sensed he was pleased with his life. President Mandela would certainly like to hear this. During Apartheid, which officially ended only five years ago, the colored race was greatly discriminated against.

While in Durban, I stayed at the Traveler's Rest hostel, a pleasant two-story wooden house with a veranda and patio. The owners, like one million other city residents, were Indian. Here, I had a surprise. Planted in front of the TV in the sitting room, was Patrick, my first Baz Bus seat companion. "What are you doing here?" I shouted embracing him like a long lost friend. "I thought you were still travelling."

Patrick returned my hug and replied, "I'm waiting for my plane back to Ireland, I got tired of traveling."

Like him, many tourists prefer to wait in Durban for their international flights out of Johannesburg. It's a safer city—less muggings, except at night—with frequent connecting flights to "Joburg".

In Durban, I switched from the Baz Bus to the Grasshopper Bus. I wanted to visit Eshowe, a small, tree shaded, colonial town in Zulu territory, which was once the center of the 1879 Anglo-Zulu war.

From my hostel, I took several tours. The first one was to Zululand, a tourist attraction. It was a Zulu kraal—a circle of beehive shaped, grass huts enclosed in a stockade—originally constructed for the film Shaka Zulu. Here I saw tribal life, met the chief, drank sorghum beer, (which tasted awful) and saw beadwork and pottery making. Then, in the evening, after dinner, I attended a dance performance. Bare-chested men in knee length, leather aprons—kicked and stomped to the sounds of women chanting and drums beating. To an outsider, it looked more like aerobics than dancing.

In Zululand I also saw a film about Zulu history.

It was their fearless king, Shaka, who made them famous. With his 50,000 ruthlessly trained warriors, he terrorized all of southern Africa. Like Napoleon, he devised ingenious battle strategies and, with his numerous conquests, carved out an empire, bigger than the size of France.

Part of Shaka's success was attributed to his new "close combat" spear—sort of like using a bigger and better mousetrap. Instead of a long, skinny spear, his warriors fought with a shorter one that had a sturdy shaft and a long broad blade. No longer did his men line up and hurl their spears "willy nilly" at the enemy, then lose them. Now, in a curved, bull-horn shaped formation, they encircled their adversaries and gorged their eyes out!

From winning his many battles, Shaka became very wealthy. Besides amassing a harem of beautiful, bead-bedecked maidens, he collected over 500,000 head of snow-white cattle, a true sign of African wealth. But in 1827, an unexpected event occurred which quickly ended his success: His beloved mother, Nandi, died causing him to suddenly "lose his marbles". In a bloody rampage he massacred 5000 mourners, and prohibited anyone, for one year, to plant crops, milk cows or even give birth. Finally, in order to end this mayhem, Shaka's half brother murdered him. For more gory details, read James Michener's book, *The Covenant,* 1200 pages.

On my second tour I visited a Zulu family who lived among brown rolling hills that stretched as far as you could see. I arrived by jeep on a rutted dirt road. Duke, the family's son in his thirties, greeted me with a traditional triple handshake (three clasps in different positions). Then, after inviting me into his parent's living room, had his mother serve me tea. The house was simply furnished. A bare light bulb hung from the ceiling and a black and white television sat on the shelf. There was no running water so his mother—it's a woman's job—had to carry it from a stream fifteen minutes away.

Behind the house stood one rondavel (hut), used strictly for ancestor worship. Here they would sit around a fire, burn incense and make offerings to the souls of the dead. No matter what they wanted, or didn't want, they consulted their ancestor's spirits about it.

In the time I spent with Duke, we talked about his life and Zulu customs. I learned that he was a night watchman and studying to be an electrician. His wife stayed at home with two of their three children. One child preferred to live with his brother. In African families this is perfectly acceptable, because cousins are treated as brothers and sisters and uncles and aunts are another set of parents.

Duke also mentioned that his father, a farmer, had a second wife (a sign of wealth). She lived elsewhere.

"I want another wife, too," he confessed, as we walked through the garden, which seemed to have more marijuana plants growing than vegetables. "But I need eleven cows for lobola, (dowry)—the going price for a bride. Now I have only three. Our chief has already promised me land for another house."

I loved my afternoon with Duke out in the peaceful countryside and thanks to him, got a glimpse of Zulu life.

PART 9

ST LUCIA; UMFOLOZI & HLUHLUWE GAME RESERVES

August (sixth week)

After Zululand, I hopped back on the Grasshopper Bus; this time heading for safari country. While on my way, something interesting happened.

It was a hazy afternoon, as we rolled along a smooth, paved highway. For no obvious reason, the driver suddenly turned off onto a dirt road. With only empty grasslands around, I wondered if he knew where he was going. For some time, we bounced along, eventually coming to some old, deserted trailers. Then, continuing farther down the road, we stopped beside a few rustic cabins sitting in a grove of trees. In the shade, stood a beautiful young girl dressed in neatly pressed khaki shorts. With her long, golden hair and slender legs, she looked like a Vogue model. To find someone so attractive running a hostel way out here in the bush was amazing. But in Africa there are always surprises!

The girl asked our driver if he had any backpackers for her. Then, she said goodbye to one of her guests who climbed on the bus carrying a shabby, leather backpack.

He was a thin man, about fifty, with rimmed glasses, unruly hair and wrinkled clothes. His narrow face had an astute expression.

For some reason, his appearance intrigued me.

Wanting to know more about him, I turned around in my seat and began talking.

"Wasn't it rather lonely out here?" I asked, thinking it would be hard for me to stay alone in such a desolate place.

"No, I liked it," he replied, looking intently into my eyes.

With an even stronger attraction to him, I continued my questions. "What did you do out here, anyway?"

"I went to a game reserve." Then he told me about the animals he had seen, mentioning that he was writing pamphlets for game parks and that he was now an ecology professor in Australia but born in South Africa.

As we continued our conversation, I felt like we were kindred souls. Besides enjoying backpacking, we shared the same love for Africa, its nature, its silence, its mysteries. We also agreed that Africa had a special spiritual quality, and being here felt like being in the center of the earth.

"You can never tame Africa," he emphasized. Then he related a story. Once, he said the government cleared some land for the people so they could plant crops and build huts. But the project failed. After a while, the wild animals returned and nature took over. Eventually the people had to leave. "Africa will always be wild," he concluded.

After an hour on the road, our driver stopped at a filling station for gas, and my new friend got off to hitch a ride to the Umlalazi game park. I was hoping he'd ask me to join him on his safari. But instead he said, "you should visit Umlalazi some time." I still regret not saying, "Well, what about now?" and courageously grabbing my backpack off the bus . . . . Oh well, I suppose I can always write for some pamphlets! I have his address.

ST. LUCIA: a resort on an estuary—home of happy hippos and lazy crocodiles.

From St. Lucia, my headquarters, I went on a safari to the Umfolozi and Hluhluwe Game Reserves.

At seven o'clock, Mike, our tour guide and driver, picked us up at the hostel, and in the early morning mist, drove us forty miles to Hluhluwe Game Reserve. After registering at the entrance, we eased slowly along a network of well-paved roads through tree-studded plains with mountains rising in the background.

Surrounded by such classical African vistas, it was hard to keep my eyes focused on finding animals. Mike, was the best in locating them; he knew just where to look. I was the worst. I depended on all the other passengers to tell me where they were. But when I did spot one of the creatures in its truly natural surroundings, going about its daily routine, I shouted with joy. It was a thrill equal to winning a ski race.

The first animals we saw were dainty tan-colored impalas with black and white markings. They ran and jumped through the thicket, like a troop of graceful dancers. Nearby stood two stoic-looking Zebra, calmly nibbling on plants, undisturbed by their frolicking neighbors. Next, my seat companion pointed out a giraffe. It was standing behind an acacia tree. All we could see was its head peering over the top of the branches—what a strange sight to see a head above a tree! Because the giraffe had dark horns, Mike told us it was a female; the males have the lighter ones.

Farther on, we noticed a small herd of water buck standing motionless in the shade. Their dark gray skin had white markings on their buttocks in the shape of a "toilet seat". By distinguishing them this way, I didn't confuse them with the gray wildebeest.

At about noon we stopped for lunch in a designated area where we were allowed to leave our van. While eating our sandwiches, we watched baboons playing in the bushes and in the river below a herd of buffalo crossing to the other shore. For the Africans, the buffalo is one of their most feared animals. Even though buffaloes eat only plants, they attack humans without provocation.

Later that afternoon, Mike took us to an area where the rhinos "hung out". To reach the observation shed, we walked through a long, narrow, enclosed, wooden corridor, with viewing slits on both sides. At the end, we sat on wooden benches in front of a small opening. There we waited silently for the rhinos. Sometimes they don't come, but we were lucky. Shortly, two enormous rhinos strolled stiff legged into our view. They wallowed in the mud and rubbed their genitals over and over on tree stumps and large rocks. All of us began to giggle and whisper remarks. Mike was annoyed at our noise and made us get quiet. "It has nothing to do with sex," he said, trying to convince us, "they're just scratching their sores and insect bites!"

As we were about to leave the Umfolozi Game Reserve, we saw two cars parked along the shoulder. Until we got closer, we couldn't figure out why. On the road right in front of them stood three, enormous elephants, weighing about 12, 000 pounds each. Immediately, Mike pulled over. Excitedly, we leaned our heads out the windows and quickly snapped pictures as they lumbered toward us. Holding our breath, we watched to see what they would do. Luckily, just before they reached us, the elephants nonchalantly veered off into the bush. "That was close!" we exclaimed, breathing a sigh of relief.

On our way back to St. Lucia, I realized that this safari was one of the highlights of my trip. It had been a perfect day.

PART 10

SWAZILAND & MOZAMBIQUE

Seventh Week

When I heard about a hostel in Swaziland where zebras grazed on the front lawn, I knew I had to go there. The hostel, called the Sondzela Lodge, was located in the middle of the Mlilwane Wildlife Sanctuary.

The trip was easy. At St. Lucia, I just jumped on the Grasshopper Bus again and in four hours we arrived at the border. Here the officials stamped our passports and welcomed us into the country.

Swaziland, like Lesotho, is a tiny kingdom. It has about 836,000 inhabitants and borders both Mozambique and South Africa. For 66 years it was ruled by the British and in 1968 became independent. Their former king—Sobhuya II who died in 1982—was known as the world's longest reigning monarch. He probably had the most wives of any known royalty, too. One hundred in all! Today one of his 200 sons rules. His name is King Mswati III.

Inside Swaziland, we traveled another hour to the wildlife sanctuary where we first registered before entering. Then as dusk was falling, we bounced along a dirt road, passing kudus, impalas and wart hogs browsing in the fields. The Sondzela Lodge sat on the edge of a range of mountains. With its overhanging straw roof, dark wood and surrounding trees, it was charming place. As I had hoped, the next morning magically produced zebras nibbling on the grass in front of the veranda.

To my surprise, the lodge was run by three, young Swazi women instead of Europeans or white South Africans as I had seen in other hostels. The reason? Swaziland never had segregation and only a few Europeans have been allowed to live in the country.

One day, in the bright afternoon sun, I took a two-hour hike to the main camp where most visitors stayed. It was unusual to be allowed to walk inside a game reserve. But since there were no lions, and since we were required to be off the path by six PM, it was considered safe.

The scenery along the trail was beautiful, mountains on one side and slopping hills on the other. I passed through the bush, inside forests and over rocks protruding out of the red soil. It was a wonderful feeling being out here all alone, spotting animals as I strolled along. I saw impalas, ostriches, baboons and vervet monkeys.

About half way on my hike, I came to a lovely lake. On a small island a crocodile was lying by a tree. Deciding to get closer for a photo, I left the path and walked on the road. Shortly, I noticed a "bigger and better" one basking in the sunshine at the water's edge. I had heard that crocodiles were dangerous animals and in spite of their short, stubby legs, could run fast. Nevertheless, the temptation to get nearer overwhelmed me. Ignoring the risk, I tip toed cautiously up behind "the croc". It was one of those times when I knew what I was doing the wrong but kept doing it anyway. When I got within 15 feet, I quickly snapped its picture, and luckily, it didn't even twitch an eyelid. Maybe it had just eaten lunch.

Only later did I realize how foolish I had been. In hurrying back to the trail, I noticed a road sign that I'd missed. It stated, "Passengers are not allowed out of their car!" No wonder the drivers stared at me!

When I arrived at the main camp, with its many tents and cabins, I sat in an open-air restaurant facing a pond. Here I watched hippos bobbing up and down in the water. They are amazing creatures. Even though they spend half of their life in the water, they can't swim. They simply walk on the bottom of the lake feeding on the vegetation. Statistically, they are Africa's most dangerous animals. Either they tip over boats or at night when they feed along the shore, attack people without warning.

PART 11

MAPUTO

At the Sondzela Lodge, everyone I met was scooting off to Mozambique—once the playground for white southern Africans. Since it was only about five hours away, I couldn't resist going, too. I got my Mozambican visa in Mbabane (the capital). Then I took the Grasshopper Bus to Manzini. From here, I rode in one of the overcrowded minibuses, known to be dangerous because of their many accidents. But I had no other choice.

On the road African women were selling vegetables and fruits in stands, just like I had seen 40 years ago when I lived in the Sudan. It was comforting to know a part of Africa hadn't changed.

Fortunately, the driver knew where Fatima's hostel was—the only backpacking one in the city—so he took me right to the door.

Maputo had a very different atmosphere from Swaziland or South Africa. Instead of English, the people spoke Portuguese, and the town had a tropical, Latin feeling to it, with espresso stands and sidewalk cafes on the streets. In spite of its relaxed ambiance, though, the city looked like it was hobbling on one leg. Its sidewalks were filled with holes, its streets dirty, its buildings shabby.

To understand why it was so poor, you need to know about Mozambique's long history of war.

First the people had to fight for their independence against the Portuguese. In 1962, Mondlane—who had an American wife—organized the Frelimos, a guerrilla army that was supported partly by the Russians and the Chinese. This army overthrew the Portuguese government and in 1975 won independence. Samora Machel of the Frelimo party then became president. Hooked on Marxist ideology, he abolished private ownership and nationalized everything, even putting the farmers in communes.

South Africa, Zimbabwe and the Portuguese were unhappy about this communist government, so they supported a rebel group, called the Renamos. As a result, the new Mozambique government had to fight another guerrilla war. It lasted 17 years. For example, when the Frelimos built schools, the Renamos would blow them up. Because of this destruction and the fact that communism wasn't working, the country's economy was soon in shambles.

In 1986 President Samora Rachel was killed in an airplane crash (President Mandela recently married his widow) so Chissano became the leader. Quickly, he dumped communism and changed the country to a market economy. In 1992, the civil war finally ended. With help from the UN, they held elections in 1994. The Frelimos won and Chissano is again the president.

After all these years of war, it's amazing that Maputo still survives.

When I complained to people about the lack of buses, the broken sidewalks and having to change money on the black market at the local tobacco store, they would say, "You should have seen this town before!" Their descriptions of the past were grim.

In spite of this, I enjoyed sightseeing in Maputo. In the daytime, I walked to the elaborate, refurbished Polano hotel that faced the Indian Ocean—a monument to colonialism; I investigated the run-down railroad station designed by Eiffel which had one train a day; I visited the revolutionary museum, where I was their only visitor and spent hours at the fabulous art museum. The Mozambicans are noted for their skill in carving wooden sculptures and painting modern art with vibrant colors and bold designs.

My evenings were spent sitting in sidewalk cafés. Here I ate sumptuous plates of seafood while bargaining with table-hopping vendors for souvenirs as well as for cashew nuts, which are grown here.

For three days I stayed in Mozambique. It was a short trip, but I was glad I had the chance to learn a little about the country and to get acquainted with its capital.

NELSPRUIT, HAZYVIEW AND KRUGER NATIONAL PARK

August: Seventh Week

To be have been in South Africa and not seen Kruger Park—the largest game reserve in Africa—seemed like visiting Paris without a trip to the Eiffel Tower. So, instead of traveling up the coast of Mozambique to join some young Australian surfers I had met, I headed back across the border and arranged a safari.

I landed at a hostel in Nelspruit. Here, the manager booked me on the 4 by 4 Tent Safari Tour out of Hazyview, about an hour away. The tour left from the Kruger Park Backpacker's Hostel, a rustic place with real African ambiance.

Krugerpark Safari truck

Krugerpark National Park

Here I stayed one night and at 5:30 AM the next morning left with two good-looking Frenchmen from Paris (lucky again) on the safari.

For two days our driver and guide, Lloyd—a young white South African with a special love for wildlife—drove the three of us around in a red and white, home-made-looking Safari truck. It was so unusual that when people weren't taking pictures of the animals, they were taking pictures of us.

I still smile when I think about it. It looked like a converted pick-up truck, built with imagination. Completely enclosed by windows, the square shell sat on top of the truck-bed and extended over the roof of the cab. We loved sitting in it, towering over everything on the road—except the giraffes. It fact, it was so tall we could stand up inside and wave to people from the front windows much like the Pope does in parades. Even our seats were unique. They were discarded airline seats.

When we reached Kruger Park at 6:00 AM, we entered by the Numbi gate, one of seven entrances. The entire 200 mile-long reserve is surrounded by a fence to keep the poachers *out* and the animals *in*.

As we cruised along that morning in the soft, pale light, Lloyd suddenly shouted from below, "Be on the look out for a rhinoceros."

"Are we in rhino territory already?" We yelled back, impressed with our guide's expertise.

"Maybe," Lloyd answered. "The piles of dung on the road means one is nearby." Then laughing, he added, "Rhinos mark their territory with their droppings."

We kept our eyes pealed on the landscape. Shortly, an enormous rhino—as big and solid as a tank—appeared by the road. We were thrilled. Rhino's are one of "the big five" that everyone wants to see and already we'd seen one of them. The others are elephants, lions, buffaloes and leopards. Personally, I like the lofty giraffes the best.

Our next exciting encounter was with a baboon. While inching along on the road (speed limit is 30km) we noticed an open safari-van coming toward us. All of a sudden a baboon jumped on a woman's lap and snatched her handbag! The van driver stopped immediately and dashed out after it. From our top window, we could see a troop of treacherous looking baboons standing by a tree ready to attack. The driver, though—being a fearless soul—completely ignored the baboon's colleagues and relentlessly chased the thief until he was able to grab back the stolen handbag. We were impressed with the driver's bravery, and I guess the other baboons were, too. They didn't even budge.

Imagine how happy the woman must have felt to see her belongings again. She was probably spared an embarrassing trip to the embassy, where she might have had to admit, "A baboon stole my passport."

By ten o'clock that morning, we arrived at the gated Szukuza rest camp, one of eighteen in the park. It was a miniature town with huts, cottages, a bank, souvenir shop, grocery store, cafeteria, post office, museum and tourist center that listed the latest lion sightings.

In a shaded picnic area we stopped for brunch. Lloyd whipped us up some fried potatoes and a tasty omelet on a gas barbecue and skillet, provided by an attendant. There were also large urns of boiling water for everyone's use. I was impressed with the modern facilities.

After eating, we set up our tents in the Szukuza camping area and spent the rest of the day driving around sighting animals. We saw elephants, hippos and crocodiles at a river; a cheetah—the swiftest animal on earth—walking down a path; some ugly hyenas devouring bones and hundreds of impalas darting around. The roads were well marked, but we had to be careful to be off of them by 6:00 PM, otherwise we would be fined.

The second day of our safari was even more thrilling than the first. As we were driving along, we came across rows and rows of cars lined up on the road, indicating something special was happening. We parked our safari truck, and to our delight, spotted a pride of lions (one male and four females) lying by a bush near us. Then gradually on the other side of the road, herds of wildebeest, impalas and zebras wandered onto the open field to graze on the grass.

With so many animals in one place, it looked like a Hollywood production. The lions, seeing the possibility for an easy meal, slowly got up and wove their way across the road, hiding behind the cars. As the animals sensed their approach, they became nervous, especially the giraffes with the best view. Once the lions reached the other side, a real drama exploded. Suddenly, in unison, at least two hundred animals thundered across the road to our side. The mass exodus was an awesome sight. The herds didn't stay long, though. The lions returned to their bush beside our truck, so they stormed back to their original grazing area.

After a short pause the lions tried again, this time sneaking more discretely across the road and concealing themselves in the bushes. We watched in suspense. Suddenly, a lion, running as fast as it could, darted out after a Zebra. Immediately, the herds rushed to our side of the rode for the second time. When the lion realized it didn't have a chance to catch the zebra, it suddenly stopped the chase and casually turned around. You'd think that with so many animals to choose from, it could have at least caught one. Being a predator obviously is not an easy life.

We wanted to stay for the finale but, after an hour of this spectacle, left to find a rest camp where we could cook our breakfast. Lloyd told us this was the most exciting hunt he'd ever encountered. We felt fortunate to have seen it.

That afternoon we returned to Szukuza camp to fold up our tents. Then before leaving Kruger Park, we followed isolated gravel roads in order to look for leopards up in the trees. Unfortunately, we didn't find any, but in the two days we saw four of the "big five" and a total of 4l different kinds of animals and birds.

Truly, it was a great safari.

PART 13

PRETORIA, VICTORIA FALLS, LIVINGSTONE

August: Eighth Week

After Kruger Park, I road the Grasshopper bus to Pretoria, a city steeped in history. Having been the capital for three different governments: the Dutch (called Boers or Afrikaners), the British and now the Africans, it was loaded with historical sites. For two days I roamed around the city visiting impressive monuments.

To understand Pretoria it helps to examine South Africa's past. Basically, its a history about the conflict between the Dutch (Boers) and the British. Since the time of colonizing (between 1648-1820), the two of them have argued about *land* and *laws*. To escape the dissention, the Boers (Dutch farmers) finally left the Cape (southern area) and in 1830 began their Great Trek north in search of land and freedom. Like our westward bound pioneers, they traveled in ox-drawn wagons, but instead of fighting Indians, they fought the Africans, mainly the Zulus and the Besothos.

These "religious, cattle-farming" Boers finally settled in the north in the region near Pretoria, called the Transvaal. They didn't have peace for long, though. In 1881, the Boer Republic fought their first war against the British. Since the Boers won, they founded the South African Republic, called ZAR. Pretoria became their capital and Paul Kruger their president. Much like President Lincoln, he had only a few years of formal education and was a strong leader. Since diamonds and gold were discovered in the Boer's area, (1869 and 1871 respectively) the British wanted control of the Transvaal. Therefore, in 1899 another war broke out. This time the Boers lost, and the British governed for the next 50 years. Then came a surprise. In 1948 everything switched back to the Boers—not because of war but because of an election. The Afrikaner's (Boer's) National Party won and ruled for the next 46 years with an iron hand. Africaans, a hybrid of Dutch, became the national language and apartheid (racial segregation) the law of the land. Only recently did the Africans get their chance. In 1994, *for the first time,* they were allowed to vote. Since they make up 76% of the country's population, their party, the ANC (African National Congress), won the election. Now, South Africa has a black government and Nelson Mandela is their president.

From this glimpse into the past, you can see why Pretoria has been on center stage in South Africa's history.

PART 14

VICTORIA FALLS

Eighth week

From Pretoria I flew on a two-hour flight to Victoria Falls, one of the great natural wonders of the world. Since the Falls were so close, I didn't want to miss them.

At the airport I rode a bus into the town of Victoria Falls. By reading The *Lonely Planet Shoestring Guide on Africa,* I knew exactly where to stay: at the Town Council Rest Camp on the main street. It had a campground as well as modestly priced accommodations for about $17 a night.

In the camp's office I plopped my heavy backpack (too many souvenirs) down on a bench and stepped up to the reservation desk. "I'd like a chalet for one," I announced, feeling weary from the oppressive heat.

Without even looking up from her desk, the receptionist barked, "We're all booked."

I felt crushed. It was one of those frustrating moments in traveling when I didn't have a clue what to do next. I had a "plan B", but I didn't like either of my choices: go to a hostel outside of town with only dorms, no doubles, or to an expensive hotel.

Feeling too hungry and exhausted to move, I hung out in the office for awhile wishing my indecisive mood would vanish. Then, suddenly an idea popped into my head. In my kindest voice, I asked the receptionist when she thought a chalet would be available.

Her response stunned me. "You can have chalet number 31 NOW."

I'll never know what changed her mind, but it was the best news I could have had. The chalet she assigned me was a small, one-room house surrounded by beautiful lawns and trees. Though the showers and toilet were in another building, I didn't mind.

That afternoon, I walked to Victoria Falls, originally discovered in 1855 by Dr. Livingstone, a Scottish missionary. Their immense size was overwhelming. (2 times higher than Niagara Falls). Tons of rushing water crashed down into a deep gorge, causing a deafening roar. A rainbow hung in the surrounding mist. Nature was truly at her best. Seeing such magnificence was an unforgettable thrill. The Africans call the Falls "the smoke that thunders".

For several hours, I strolled along the mile-long path facing the Falls. Every view was breath taking.

A few days later I visited the Zambia side of the Falls. Renting a bicycle, I barreled across the border. It was a short trip, just over the bridge on the Zambezi River with a couple of custom stops. On this side, Victoria Falls was equally impressive. Enormous torrents of water rushed over the craggy cliffs, falling into the deep, narrow chasm.

From here I wanted to cycle into the town of Livingstone, only 12 miles away. All the park rangers, though—as well as the souvenir vendors—said it was too dangerous. "There may be robbers along the way," they warned me.

Reluctantly, I gave up the idea and headed for a taxi. Just as I got near, it filled up and left. Then I waited for a bus. As soon as I climbed on, it had a flat tire.

With no bike, no taxi, no bus and no luck, I decided to stand along the road and wave down one of the few passing cars. Finally, an open safari jeep screeched to a halt, and the African driver and his European lady passenger offered me a ride. Grateful to escape the sizzling heat, I climbed in.

Farther down the road, we picked up another passenger—this time, a tall, young Zambian man in his twenties, named Oliver. As we got acquainted, he told me his job was traveling back and forth to South Africa to bring back manufactured goods. He was a pleasant fellow. When I got off at the Livingstone museum, he volunteered to accompany me. I was glad he did. From his explanations, I learned that Zambia has only nine million inhabitants, got its independence from the British as early as 1964 and because there is no longer a market for its copper, has a poor economy.

Later Oliver and I walked into the center of Livingstone—a dusty, drowsy looking town with few people on the streets and shabby merchandise in the shops. A feeling of poverty hung in the air.

We ate lunch in a small café (chicken pies and rice) then Oliver accompanied me to the bus station. By late afternoon, I was back at the Zimbabwe border—safe and sound—and pleased with my day's adventure.

Because there was so much to do in Victoria Falls, I stayed a whole week. It had elegant dining at first class hotels, an evening tribal dance program, a craft village showing huts from different tribes, a sunset cruise on the Zambezi River, a crocodile farm, a game reserve, great souvenir shopping and more. Of all these attractions, I liked my cycling along the Zambezi River the best.

One morning, under a teal blue sky, I pedaled along on a shaded path at the river's edge, stopping frequently under palm trees to soak up the lush beauty. Quiet and calm, the Zambezi River reminded me of the Nile, by whose banks I once lived.

As I was gliding leisurely along near the end of the three mile trail, I heard the crackling of branches. Looking up at the trees, I saw two elephants about 25 feet away. I was scared to death. Never had I expected to see elephants on my trail! With my heart pounding, I watched breathlessly to see what they would do. To my relief, one turned and sauntered down the path—fortunately not in my direction. The other one continued munching on leaves. I snapped a few photos and disappeared as quickly as I could. Needless to say, this encounter made my day!

PART 15

MAUN & OKAVANGO DELTA, A WORLD FAMOUS DELTA.

September: Tenth Week

From Victoria Falls I planned to visit the Okavango Delta of Botswana, the largest inland delta in the world. My problem was, though, I couldn't figure out how to get there.

Boat ride at A Makoro

One travel agent recommended that I join an expensive $400-a-day-tour, which I couldn't afford, of course. Other backpackers suggested I hitchhike or ride in an overland truck for three days—unappealing options to say the least. Even the *Lonely Planet Guide*—my bible—never mentioned transportation between the two places. Still, I knew, there must be a way.

Then one day, while waiting in line at the "Vic" Falls post office, I heard a customer say that Botswana Airlines had a new flight to Maun, the town nearest the delta. Elated by the good news, I darted off to the airline office and quickly purchased a ticket. And what a bargain! Only seventy-five dollars!

Next I needed to find a reasonable mokoro (African canoe) trip into the Okavango Delta. Confident there would be a way, I began asking the passengers at the "Vic" Falls airport about their delta plans from Maun. Luckily, through my inquires, I met Hans and Mark, two middle-aged Germans. They had made their Okavango reservations six months ago and knew just where to go. God bless German efficiency!

At the Maun airport they introduced me to their travel agent. I told her I wanted to take the same trip as my new friends. By short wave radio, she contacted the Oddball Lodge in the delta and in a few hours everything was arranged, verifying my old theory that there's usually room for one more!

The next morning the three of us met on the Maun runway and, with six other passengers, boarded a tiny bush plane. A pretty, young Australian woman flew us low over the Okavango River (third longest in Africa). From a crystal clear, blue sky we had a panoramic view of a maze of meandering waterways crisscrossing the dry, flat plains. It was a fantastic sight, especially with animals roaming the shores. From our plane, the herds of buffaloes looked like swarms of ants.

Water seeps into the delta from the Okavango River. It begins in Angola and spreads its long fingers through miles and miles of grasslands, eventually disappearing into the greedy sands of the Kalahari Desert. The Africans call it "a river that never finds the sea."

After forty minutes in the air, we skidded to a spine-jolting stop on an airstrip (term used loosely—more like a bumpy field). The "well-heeled" passengers walked only a few yards to the posh Delta Lodge at the river's edge. The rest of us, under a scorching mid-day sun, hiked for twenty-minutes with a guide to the Oddball Lodge.

Sitting high on stilts, the lodge faced the calm Okavango River. From a large wooden veranda we could see a variety of wildlife pass by: elephants crossing the river, hippos bobbing up and down, impalas jumping and sprinting along the river's banks. The location was perfect.

Peter, the owner—a tall, slender, about forty man with unusual, piercing green eyes—had a friendly, relaxed manner that made us feel instantly welcome. He first lectured to us about being careful of the wild animals in the camp, then assigned us to individual tents among the trees. They were erected on platforms and equipped with mattresses, sleeping bags and a couple of chairs.

Later, I understood his warning. While I was in the shower, I heard a strange noise, as if someone were shaking trees. I went out to investigate and could hardly believe my eyes. Just a few feet away stood an enormous elephant munching on the fallen palm nuts off the ground.

Joining the other spectators, I followed the elephant around the camp, watching it shake every palm tree it could fine. When it had exhausted the supply of nuts, it performed a most amazing feat. Placing its long trunk vertically along the trunk of a towering tree, it gave one big push. With a loud crash, the tree came tumbling down, carefully missing a nearby tent. Now it could tear off the leaves with ease, without reaching up so high. "It's a frequent visitor to our camp," Peter commented, surprisingly unconcerned about the uprooted tree.

The next morning Hans, Mark and I began our delta trip. I was in one mokoro—a narrow, dugout canoe—and they were in another. Maiketso (I called him Mike) my poler and guide, provided the tents, sleeping bags and cooking equipment, and I bought our canned food and bottled water from Oddball's store.

Mike poled me along in the shallow water by standing up in the back and lifting his ten-foot pole back and forth with the graceful motion of a gondolier. We eased along through streams, lakes, canals, lagoons and ponds of water lilies. It was a marvelous trip. I felt like Cleopatra being chauffeured down the Nile.

Our polers, when possible, stayed close to shore, in case hippos or crocodiles were lurking underneath the water, scheming to capsize our mokoros. One time, while threading our way through a field of tall reeds, a loud splash suddenly ripped the stillness. In a clearing just ahead, two buffaloes stood in our path staring at us with their mean, suspicious eyes. Our polers froze. I could tell they were as scared as I was. Cautiously, without a sound, they backed up our mokoros. It was a very tense moment. No one moved. Would they charge at us? We waited. At last, realizing we were not a threat, they turned and disappeared. Flirting with danger is one of Africa's attractions! It makes good photos, too!

After riding for four hours, we docked along side an island and set up our tents underneath a large, shady tree. It was a wonderful campsite, right in the heart of raw wilderness—savage and untamed. Across from our camp, on the other side of a marsh, herds of impala gathered from time to time. As soon as we moved or talked, though, they'd disappear.

I loved the night. In the darkness and under a ceiling of sparkling stars, Africa spoke with another voice. Nocturnal sounds pierced the deep, immense silence, and. the air filled with a symphony of exotic sounds. I was excited and frightened at the same time. Did the roars, grunts and screeches mean that the animals were far or near? And was I safe inside my tent? Mike always assured me that our all-night-fire would scare wildlife away. I prayed he was right!!!!!

Twice a day, in the early morning dawn and before dusk fell, Mike (unarmed) would take me on a two-to-three hour walking safari into the vast open plains dotted with trees. It was an immense thrill spotting the animals as we strolled along. But, unlike in a vehicle, we could never get close to them. Our scent, movement and noise scared them away.

I learned many things about the bush. Mike taught me how to scan the tawny grasslands for the camouflaged creatures and how to recognize their footprints and droppings. One time, pointing at footprints the size of a large pancake, he observed, "Those from angry elephant."

"How do you know he's angry?" I asked curiously.

"It has baby."

Another time, after seeing a family of giraffes, I mentioned that they were my favorite animals. "What are yours?" I asked.

His response astounded me. "I hate wild animals. They just for tourists," he complained in a bitter voice. "Government spends too much money on game parks. I want cows. I can support family with cows."

Being a tourist, I was sorry to hear this.

After three days in these peaceful surroundings, Mike poled me back to the Oddball Lodge. I stayed a while longer there, wishing I never had to leave.

PART 16

WINDHOEK, SWAKOPMUND, SOSSUSVLEI (SAND DUNES)

September: Eleventh Week

All the tourists and backpackers I met raved about Namibia. After discovering it sat on Botswana's doorstep, I squeezed it in to my itinerary.

Sand Dunes in Namibia

From Maun, I flew directly to Windhoek, Namibia's capital that sits on a flat, arid plain, with tall buildings extending like fingers into the sky. It was a modern city of 161, 000 inhabitants, alive with German influence. On the main street were half-timbered stores, a clock tower and restaurants advertising sumptuous Wiener schnitzel and bratwurst. Even the merchants in the shops spoke German.

German influence seeped into the continent when the European nations began their untamed colonizing of the world. In the late 1800's Germany grabbed Namibia, then called South West Africa. But it didn't rule the country for long. After World War 1 the League of Nations gave it to South Africa. Not until 1984 did Namibia's one and a half million inhabitants win their independence. Even today, you can feel touches of South Africa's presence. They still use the Rand. While in Namibia, I wanted to see Sossusvlei's ever shifting sand dunes, known to be the highest in the world. Since no public transport was available, I joined a tour from the town of Swakopmund on the foggy Atlantic Ocean—a four hour bus trip from Windhoek (windy corner) across a dry, barren desert.

At Swakopmund's municipal rest camp, I rented a small bungalow for one night, complete with kitchen and bath. It wasn't anything fancy but a real bargain for $17 a night and located only four blocks from the ocean.

Swakopmund was a tourist's playground. It had half moon beaches, attractive buildings decorated with colorful, ornate facades and turrets and many other attractions: a new aquarium, a fascinating museum, a fishing pier, palm-lined promenades, seaside cafes and elegant hotels where Michael Jackson and other American celebrities were supposed to have stayed.

The next morning I joined my tour. My fellow travelers were young couples from Italy, England, Holland and Austria, and our driver/guide was an extremely capable girl. Not only was she a good organizer and cook but also knew how to repair our van when it broke down. Her efficient, Germanic manner kept us all in line. No one dared be late!

Our first stop that morning was at a bird sanctuary at Walvis Bay. Here thousands of pink Flamingos stood motionless in a blue lagoon. After seeing this unforgettable sight, we turned inland and for the next five hours jostled along on a rutted, gravel road. All the European passengers, being from crowded countries, were enthralled with the endless space and harsh desert landscape. As for me, I felt I had never left California.

That night, in a campground in the bleak Namib Desert, we pitched our sturdy canvas tents and at 5:00 A.M. the next morning piled into the van—half asleep—for a two-hour drive to Sossusvlei. From the parking lot there, we hiked in the clear, fresh air for three miles to the bottom of the dunes.

Climbing up in the fine, deep sand was much more difficult than I had anticipated. We had to crawl on our hands and knees to reach the top of the first dune. Once on a ridge, it was a little easier to walk, that is as long as we followed in someone's footprints and didn't fall off the narrow edge; otherwise, we had the unpleasant task of crawling back up again.

With hearts pounding, we stopped regularly to catch our breaths and soak up nature's magnificent splendor. As far as we could see, a sea of pinkish, brown dunes spread before us. Then, as the sun climbed higher in the sky, the landscape turned a gorgeous apricot shade.

After laboring for two hours with every step, we reached the summit of the highest dune, about 1000 feet. Exhausted but exhilarated, we gazed at even more extensive views.

Fearing our descent would be another struggle, I felt greatly relieved when it turned out to be a "blast". Barefooted, we ran down the steep mountain of sand, feeling free like a bird. If we plunged into the deep sand, it didn't matter; it was as soft as feathers.

At the bottom of the dune sat a dried-up lakebed, called a pan. Its white, mosaic cracked surface, dotted with dead, black tree trunks, gave it an eiry, surrealistic look. Walking on its lifeless, moon-like crust made me feel that I was on the edge of another reality. On the other side, we ascended more dunes, now a rich orange tint from the bright sunshine. This spectacular panorama took my breath away and so did climbing up more steep dunes.

Even though our hike was long and strenuous, the dramatic views made the effort worth while.

PART 17

JOHANESBURG

From Namibia I flew back to South Africa. Before leaving, I wanted to see Johannesburg, even though I knew that I might be stepping into a minefield. (The city has the reputation of being the most dangerous city in the world.)

At the airport, I phoned the highly recommended Ritz Backpacker's Hostel. At no charge, they sent a driver to pick me up.

I was relieved to find the hostel sat in a safe, affluent suburb. All the neighbors on the street had mansions with private pools and tennis courts. Our hostel was a huge estate, too. Encircled by tall trees, lush gardens and a lawn with a large swimming pool, it once belonged to a general who during the Anglo-Boer war in 1899 used its stone towers as a fortress.

While in Johannesburg, I wanted to visit the downtown area. But when I asked the desk clerk how to get there, she exclaimed, "Do you want to be *killed*! The hotels and shops are all closed. There's nothing to see."

To avoid any messy encounter with death at this stage in my life, I changed my plans. Instead, I joined a tour to Soweto, a town on the other side of the city where 5 million blacks live.

Our guide first led us through the poorest area, a shantytown with dilapidated shacks, crowded closely together along narrow, smelly dirt paths. Here the Africans live in abominable conditions with only public pit toilets, no electricity or running water in their shacks and only a few outside water facets. I felt depressed seeing "life" in the grips of hopeless poverty.

Later, we saw other neighborhoods with small, individual houses. They, too, looked poor with only dirt around them, no lawns, trees or flowers anywhere. Then at the end of our tour, we passed by President Mandela's former house, now a museum, and Winnie Mandela's present home.

Originally, I had planned to stay five days in Johannesburg. But after experiencing "traveler's burnout", I decided to return a few days early to visit my friend, Teresa, in England. In retrospect, this was a poor decision.

London turned out to be even *more dangerous* than Africa. While there, I was hit on the head with a flowerpot.

Walking under the wrong window? Not at all.

All I was doing was sitting in Teresa's apartment in the Wrong chair. It happened to be next to a six feet tall bookcase where a flowerpot was holding up some books on the top shelf. While stuffing an atlas back on this shelf, Teresa accidentally knocked over the books and down came the flowerpot on top of my head.—only suppose to happen in movies, right?

In spite of this cruel hand of fate and a "gnarly" concussion, my trip was still fabulous experience. The mystique of Africa captured my soul!

ABOUT THE AUTHOR

The purpose of my life has been to see the world. I have spent most of my life traveling around the world in different ways. It started just after graduating from Berkeley in 1950. My first trip was to Germany working as a recreational director for Special Services. Later I traveled to Japan with the same organization. I then would go to different locations and hold jobs (usually teaching English,) and stay for extended periods of time this covered about the next 10 years of my life. I took a break to raise two sons but was able to travel here and there. During this time as a foreign language teacher (French, Spanish and German) I received a yearlong sabbatical in Gladbeck, Germany to study German and teach English. My entire family went with me. Three years later I received a second sabbatical to study French in Normandy. We immersed ourselves into the French and German lifestyle for an entire year.

When my sons went off to college, and I was single again, I joined the Peace Corps in Thailand where I taught English at Songhla University. After a year I resigned from Peace Corps and left for China where I taught in Nanchong. I loved living here. My next stops were Hong Kong, Singapore, Bali, India and Africa.

When I returned home as my boys graduated college, I substituted and rented my house to cover my summer trips and month long winter ski trips. I always traveled alone with a backpack, good maps and travel books. I did this for about 8-10 years visiting the remaining places that I have longed to visit like Africa and the Middle East, Croatia, to name a few. This book contains two of my traveling experiences to Turkey and the Middle East. On this trip I had some fascinating experiences and good adventures which I thought others might enjoy reading about.

Then in my 60's I started on my third variation of traveling, by bicycle. I began in California first in the south west then in the North West to gain experience and settle on the supplies that I would take on my new trips. This involved shipping my big load of equipment, tent, sleeping bag and whatever else I needed. Over the next 7 summers I experienced some of the most enjoyable times traveling on my bicycle. I rode the dikes of Holland, the wine country of Italy, canals of France and rivers of Germany. For some of these trips I have written about my experiences in the following books : *Canals of France* and *a Life of Travel and* Adventure.